WILLIAMSPORT
BOOMTOWN ON THE SUSQUEHANNA

Returning World War I veterans march under a Victory Arch on West Fourth Street at the Williamsport Sun-Gazette *Building and the building that is today City Hall. (JVBL.)*

THE
MAKING OF AMERICA
SERIES

WILLIAMSPORT
BOOMTOWN ON THE SUSQUEHANNA

ROBIN VAN AUKEN AND
LOUIS HUNSINGER, JR.

ARCADIA
PUBLISHING

ISBN 978-0-7385-2438-2

Published by Arcadia Publishing
Charleston, South Carolina

Printed in the United States of America

Library of Congress control number: 2003106992

For all general information contact Arcadia Publishing at:
Telephone 843-853-2070
Fax 843-853-0044
E-mail sales@arcadiapublishing.com
For customer service and orders:
Toll-Free 1-888-313-2665

Visit us on the Internet at www.arcadiapublishing.com

DEDICATION:

FOR LANCE, SARAH, AND LANCE

FOR DORIS AND LOU SR.

Front cover: *This view shows the curbstone market on market day, looking north from Market Square in the 1880s or 1890s. An unlikely success, the curbstone market became a thriving industry in Williamsport. (LCHS.)*

Contents

ACKNOWLEDGMENTS

A historical account can be fraught with misinterpretations, and often will bypass the contributions of many. It is with this handicap that we embarked on this collective effort, knowing that along the way thousands of people (particularly women, and Native and African Americans) would be devalued. Not because they are not fundamental in the annals of history, but because they—like the millions who came before and after—have been slighted in the retelling.

We would like to acknowledge the nameless, faceless pioneers of Williamsport, and beyond, in hopes that in the future every effort to record history accurately, regardless of gender or ethnicity, will be made.

We are most grateful to several individuals, organizations, and institutions for their valuable support in the making of *Williamsport: Boomtown on the Susquehanna*.

We are particularly appreciative for the use of the *Williamsport Sun-Gazette*'s photographic (including *The Grit*) and news archives (WSG/GRIT). Our thanks to publisher John Yahner and editor Dave Troisi for their generosity and support.

From the Lycoming County Historical Society, we are indebted to Jack Buckle, photograph collections curator, for guiding us through the society's extensive holdings, and to Sandra Rife, executive director, for her invaluable stewardship of the county's history and allowing us the opportunity to explore it (LCHS).

Our heartfelt thanks are owed to the staff of the James V. Brown Library, a treasure in downtown Williamsport. Not only is it a pleasure to use this wonderful institution's resources, our multiple visits have been joyous because of the delightful reference librarians and their constant support and interest. Gratitude is owed to executive director Janice Trapp, and librarians Helen Yoas, Tricia Haas, Nancy Shipley, Wanda Bower, Beth Albertini, Linda Aston, Mary Buchanan, and Rosemary Heffner (JVBL).

We would like to thank Stephen D. Keener of Little League Baseball, Inc., whose collection of photographs by Putsee Vannucci is unrivaled (LLB).

Finally, we need to recognize Lance Van Auken for his invaluable editorial skills, historical advice, and loyalty.

—Robin Van Auken and Louis Hunsinger Jr.
Williamsport, PA

INTRODUCTION

Williamsport, Pennsylvania is a small metropolis with a dramatic history. Famous throughout the world for its impressive forest products, it once boasted more millionaires per capita than any American city. A hale and hearty pioneer village on the West Branch of the Susquehanna River, early settlers found a wild and romantic region and a thriving Indian population.

Covered with an abundance of large timber, the virgin forests contained the finest hemlock and white pine. European settlers cut logs for a twofold purpose: to build cabins and to clear land. After their homes were built, the pioneers looked upon the standing timber as a liability instead of an asset. Many miles of forest were burned as the land was cleared. Soon, however, the need for finished lumber arose and the first sawmills were erected.

Booms were built to divert the logs down the river as a developing New World clamored for sawed timber. Williamsport, the lumber capital of the continent, was more than willing to provide. From 1862 to 1894, lumber was "King." At the peak of the era, more than 1.5 million logs were cut from the mountain slopes annually. Transportation evolved from rafts to canal boats, which soon were replaced by the railroad. Williamsport thrived and industry grew.

Inevitably, the mountainsides were denuded, forest fires ran unchecked, and disastrous floods toppled the lumbering companies. Its heyday over, Williamsport declined and the inhabitants used the cleared land for agriculture.

In 1939, however, the world once again heard from Williamsport after a humble young man developed the Little League Baseball program. Each year, thousands of people make the pilgrimage to the small mountainous region to watch young children play baseball during the Little League Baseball World Series. Millions more watch the games on television. An international event, Little League is found in places like Bosnia and Herzegovina, South Africa, Taiwan, Australia, Venezuela, Israel, and all 50 U.S. states.

Williamsport: Boomtown on the Susquehanna is based in part upon research developed by the authors for the successful newspaper series "History Shapers of Lycoming County," published by the *Williamsport Sun-Gazette* from 1999 to 2000. It is a glimpse of the city's tumultuous origin, beginning with the prehistory of the region and its early settlers and city founders, and examining the irenic days following the termination of the Native American population. Most important is the lumber boom and meteoric rise of the community as millions of dollars flooded the economy. The authors examine the collapse of the boom, the region's transition from lumber to agriculture, the city's struggle through war and depression, and its stagnant post-industrial era.

The authors also examine the city's future. Its heritage and creative community may be the very thing that liberates Williamsport, as its city planners look to the future with extensive downtown redevelopment and promotion of its natural beauty.

Williamsport has suffered the rise and decline of most small towns, but it continues to strive to protect and preserve its cultural heritage. Its citizens remain proud of its majestic mountains and narrow gorges, contrasting with beautiful valleys and fertile farmland. Perhaps as a harbinger of its rebirth, the area's protected forests are once again dense with pine and hemlock, surrounding the meandering streams and picturesque waterfalls that made it such a desirable destination in its heyday.

The Centennial Exposition Building was constructed to celebrate the centennial of Lycoming County in 1895. It was located on Pine Street near the Pine Street United Methodist Church and used to display products and the history of Lycoming County. (JVBL.)

1. Prehistory of the Susquehanna West Branch Valley

Before the coming of European traders and settlers, Indians skillfully managed the natural bounty of the Susquehanna River region by living in accordance with the seasons. They hunted, fished, gathered nuts, berries, and other wild foods, and cultivated corn, beans, and squash.

Before European contact, the areas now known as Lycoming County and Williamsport were inhabited in turn by two prehistoric Indian groups: the Iroquois and the Algonquin. The powerful Iroquois organized a confederacy known as the Six Nations, which consisted of the Seneca, Cayuga, Oneida, Onodaga, Mohawk, and Tuscarora.

When discovered by Europeans, Indian groups reflected a Stone Age background, especially in material arts and crafts. Tools, weapons, and household equipment were made from stone, wood, and bark. People traveled on foot or by canoe. Houses were made of bark. Clothing came from the skins of animals. The rudiments of a more complex civilization were at hand in the arts of weaving, pottery, and agriculture, although hunting and food gathering prevailed.

Another large linguistic group in Pennsylvania was the Algonkian, represented by the Delaware, Shawnee, and other tribes. The Delaware, calling themselves Leni-Lenape, or "real people," originally occupied the basin of the Delaware River and were the most important of several tribes that spoke an Algonkian language. Under the pressure of white settlement, they began to drift westward to the Wyoming Valley, to the Allegheny, and finally to eastern Ohio.

The Susquehannock people, also known as the Andaste, lived along the West Branch of the Susquehanna River. In the Algonkian-speaking tribes' territory, the Susquehannocks engaged in many wars and suffered from diseases brought by European settlers. The Iroquois destroyed them as a nation by 1675, and their lineage ended in 1763 after a few survivors were massacred along with the Conestoga Indians of Lancaster County.

Archaeologist James Bressler visits the Heritage Park named in his honor. Located on Canfield Island, the park contains a significant prehistoric Indian village in Loyalsock Township. Bressler has excavated the island for many decades and is responsible for having the island listed with the National Register of Historic Places. (WSG/GRIT.)

MADAM MONTOUR: INDIAN TRADER AND TRANSLATOR

New World history—and especially that of the Susquehanna Valley—is filled with tales of "rugged pioneers" and "bloodthirsty savages," and one of the more interesting is Madam Montour. Reliable details of her life are sketchy, but are mythic in proportion. Historians have proposed that Elizabeth Catherine "Madam" Montour led an adventurous life on the French and English frontiers.

Montour was born in 1667 at Three Rivers, Canada, the daughter of Frenchman Pierre Couc and his Algonkian wife, whose name is unknown. According to Dr. Paul Wallace, historian and former consultant to the Pennsylvania Historical and Museum Commission, Madam Montour spent several years in the early 1700s at Forts Mackinac and Detroit, Michigan, where her relatives were engaged in the Indian trade. John G. Freeze, in an 1879 article published in the *Pennsylvania Magazine of History and Biography*, reports that she married Roland Montour, "a brave of the Senecas." No further information is available about him.

In 1709, while conducting Native Americans to trade in Albany, her brother Louis, an interpreter, was murdered. Madam Montour, who had accompanied Louis, remained in New York and, because of her knowledge of various European and Indian languages, was employed by Governor Robert Hunter as an interpreter. There she married an Oneida chief, Carondowana. In 1727, when the Oneida Chief Swatana (Shikellamy) came to Pennsylvania, Madam Montour and her family came also. She again served as an interpreter until her husband was killed in a 1729 raid.

Alison D. Hirsch, assistant professor of American studies and history at Penn State University, writing on Madam Montour, claims she stands out in American history as a "self-fashioned woman . . . the most creative—most outrageous—in fashioning her life from the whole cloth in the midst of Pennsylvania's most volatile frontiers."

Evidently illiterate, Madam Montour never signed any document with more than an "X" and historians must rely on sparse records by others. She allowed Pennsylvanians to believe that her parents were French and her father was a governor of Canada. Her myth included that she had been captured at a young age and raised among the Native Americans. She spoke English, German, Algonquin, and Iroquois, as well as French.

According to historical reports, Madam Montour lived near present-day Montoursville with her son Andrew and her niece French Margaret. Her village, Otstonwakin, was essentially a Delaware (Lenape) town. Established around 1728, the village was deserted by 1755, the villagers suffering from a smallpox epidemic.

In John F. Meginness's *History of Lycoming County*, Count Nikolaus Ludwig Graf Von Zinzendorf, a Moravian missionary in Pennsylvania traveling with Conrad Weiser, recounts in his journal a meeting with Madam Montour in 1742:

> The journal kept by Count Zinzendorf shows his party left Shamokin for the upper reaches of the West Branch on Sept. 30, 1742. When they approached Otstuagy (Montoursville)—sometimes called Otstonwakin—Weiser rode ahead to notify the inhabitants. It was then the residence of the celebrated Madam Montour, a French half-breed who located there as early as 1727.

Witham Marshe interviewed Madam Montour in 1744, reporting that at the age of 77 she was a "handsome woman, genteel and of polite address." She died in 1753.

Zinzendorf describes her son Andrew as a guide and interpreter whose

> cast of countenance is decidedly European, and had his face not been encircled with a broad band of paint, applied with bear's fat, I would certainly have taken him for one. He wore a brown broadcloth coat, a scarlet damask lapel waistcoat, breeches over which his shirt hung, a black Cordovan neckerchief decked with silver bangles, shoes and stockings, and a hat. He was very cordial, but on addressing him in French, he, to my surprise, replied in English.

Zinzendorf also reports that Andrew Montour's ears were "braided with brass and other wire like a handle on a basket."

According to historian Paul Wallace, Andrew Montour performed numerous diplomatic errands for both Pennsylvania and Ohio, and held a captain's commission from Virginia in 1754. Montour also received (but did not keep) land in present-day Mifflin County and Montoursville. A Seneca Indian killed him near Pittsburgh in 1772.

French Margaret moved into the West Branch Valley from the Allegheny River area in 1745. According to Meginness, Madam Montour's niece established a town—and enforced prohibition—within the present limits of Williamsport's 7th Ward.

Moravian evangelist John Martin Mack visited French Margaret's Town in 1753, and writes the following in his journal:

> Aug. 28—Towards 9 a.m. we came to a small town where Madam Montour's niece Margaret lives with her family. She welcomed us cordially, led us into the hut, and set before us milk and watermelons. We had a long conversation with her on many subjects. She spoke of her husband (a Mohawk Indian known as Peter Quebec) who has had no whiskey for six years and who has already dissuaded two men from drinking. French Margaret is held in high esteem by the Indians, and allows no drunkards in her town.

Indian Vengeance

During the turbulent years leading up to the French and Indian War, settlers in Northcentral Pennsylvania had two choices: they could leave the fertile valleys of the Susquehanna, or take their chances with sporadic Native American raids during which farms were destroyed and entire families slaughtered.

Penn's Creek settlers were the first to experience "the effects of Indian vengeance" on October 15, 1755. Frustrated with white settlers who continued to work their way westward, "a hostile body of savages, painted and clad in war costume, descended the West Branch and fell upon the Penn's Creek settlements," Meginness writes. "Every person in the settlement—25 men, women and children—were either killed or carried into captivity. The cabins were burned, stock slain and fields laid waste. We are particular in noting this first massacre, for it marks the beginning of the long French and Indian War which followed, and in which the settlers of this portion (present-day Lycoming County) suffered so severely."

The massacre was the first to occur in the Province of Pennsylvania east of the Alleghenies and terrorized the other settlements along the river.

Two weeks later, Andrew Montour and old Chief Monagatootha were summoned by a band of Delaware and Shawnee Indians and were told of plans by the French to kill and scalp settlers. The Delaware asked them to unite in a war against the English, but Montour and Chief Monagatootha declined. According to Meginness, Montour reported this intelligence to Governor Robert H. Morris; however, the governor was indifferent to frontier conflicts at the time.

John Meginness, the author of the monumental History of Lycoming County *and a former editor for the* Gazette and Bulletin, *also wrote* Otsinachson, *an Indian name for the Susquehanna River, in 1855, after conducting exhaustive research and financing its publication with his money. (JVBL.)*

WAR IS DECLARED ON DELAWARE INDIANS

After repeated attacks on settlers and continued unrest, Governor Morris, on April 14, 1756, issued a declaration of war against the Delaware tribe and others in confederacy with them. The declaration of war, Zimmerman counters, was economically motivated, not because of murdered settlers: "From the Mother Country's point of view, Indian affairs are the most important type of entry listed . . . and the conflict with the French in the Ohio Valley, brought about by the Pennsylvania trader, triggered for Britain a world-wide war effort."

Governor Morris issued a statement naming the Delaware Indians and their allies "enemies, rebels and traitors to His Most Sacred Majesty," and required all subjects of the province to pursue and kill them.

He posted a "Reward for Indian Scalps," Meginness writes, "thinking no doubt that bombast would immediately frighten the Delawares into peaceful submission." He offered £150 for every adult male Native American prisoner above 12 years of age; 130 for the scalp of every male enemy (with proof of death); 130 for every female prisoner and male prisoner under 12 years; and 50 for the scalp of every female Native American enemy. The announcement caused much excitement among the people, and in particular, it distressed the Quakers, "whose sympathies were with the savages," Meginness reports. He further claims that Morris's proclamation

> was too bombastic to have a good effect, and had he ordered defensive movements sooner and threatened less, he might have accomplished

> more important results and saved the scalp of many a white settler. As it was feared, his proclamation only intensified the vindictive feelings of the Indians and caused them to commit greater atrocities.

The British began work on Fort Augusta, which became an important factor in the early settlement of the West Branch region and the place of refuge for many a settler flying from what is now Lycoming County to "escape the tomahawk and scalping knife. [Lycoming County] was constantly infested with roving bands of savages bent on pillage and murder."

Present-day Lycoming County was far removed from the battlefields of recent history, yet the French considered the West Branch Valley an important route and attempted an invasion here. Before Fort Augusta was complete, a French expedition to overtake it was recorded by Marquis de Vaudreuil on July 13, 1757, and is in the Archives of France.

French soldier M. De St. Ours, along with six Canadians and fourteen Indians, traveled down the Susquehanna to the mouth of the Loyalsock. A scouting party took two scalps outside Fort Augusta. Dissuaded, however, by reports of the garrison's strength, the invaders withdrew without formally attacking, purportedly dumping their cannon downstream of the Loyalsock. Archaeological evidence supports the brief stay of French in the area.

Bounties for Scalps

According to George A. Bray III in "The Delicate Art of Scalping," history is replete with incidents of scalping by French, English, and Native American combatants. He writes, "Scalping, of course, predated the mid-18th century. Historical records, archaeology and other sciences strongly indicate the practice originated among certain Native American tribes."

Bray found in the memoirs of a French soldier, identified by the initials J.C.B., a description of a scalping:

> When a war party has captured one or more prisoners that cannot be taken away, it is the usual custom to kill them by breaking their heads with the blows of a tomahawk. When he has struck two or three blows, the savage quickly seizes his knife, and makes an incision around the hair from the upper part of the forehead to the back of the neck. Then he puts his foot on the shoulder of the victim, whom he has turned over face down, and pulls the hair off with both hands, from back to front. This hasty operation is no sooner finished than the savage fastens the scalp to his belt and goes on his way. This method is only used when the prisoner cannot follow his captor. When a savage has taken a scalp, and is not afraid he is being pursued, he stops and scrapes the skin to remove the blood and fibers on it. He makes a hoop of green wood, stretches the skin over it like a tambourine, and puts it in the sun to dry a little.

> The skin is painted red, and the hair on the outside combed. When prepared, the scalp is fastened to the end of a long stick, and carried on his shoulder in triumph to the village or place where he wants to put it. But as he nears each place on his way, he gives as many cries as he has scalps to announce his arrival and show his bravery. Sometimes as many as 15 scalps are fastened on the same stick. When there are too many for one stick, they decorate several sticks with the scalps.

Bray recounts another description of scalping from the memoirs of Captain Pierre Pouchot of the Bearn Regiment, who was commandant at Fort Niagara for most of the war:

> As soon as the man is felled, they run up to him, thrust their knee in between his shoulder blades, seize a tuft of hair in one hand and, with their knife in the other, cut around the skin of the head and pull the whole piece away. The whole thing is done very expeditiously. Then, brandishing the scalp, they utter a whoop, which they call the death whoop. If they are not under pressure and the victory has cost them lives, they behave in an extremely cruel manner towards those they kill or the dead bodies. They disembowel them and smear their blood all over themselves.

It is important to remember, Bray writes, that while Europeans did not originate scalping, they advocated it through the establishment of bounties and "the French and English were accustomed to pay for the scalps, to the amount of 30 francs' worth of trade goods. Their purpose was then to encourage the savages to take as many scalps as they could and to know the number of the foe who had fallen."

The French preferred to purchase prisoners that they would at times send back to their families or utilize for prisoner exchanges. Father Pierre Joseph Antonie Roubaud, missionary to the Abenaki at St. Francis, obtained a scalp from one of his warriors to redeem an infant from a Huron captor. The priest then reunited him with his parents.

The English passed acts through their colonial assemblies encouraging the practice. Even before war was declared and before Governor Morris offered to pay for enemy scalps, Massachusetts Governor William Shirley offered £40 for Native American male scalps and £20 for female scalps.

Some entrepreneurs came up with the idea of ersatz scalps, made of horsehide, which they prepared in the same way as human scalps. The fraud's discovery resulted in more careful inspections before payment was made. Friendly Indians were often killed by ambush simply for the reward, so the French and English eventually paid only a trifling amount in the form of presents.

There were actually times when people survived the experience. The *New York Gazette* of July 30, 1759, carried an article proclaiming, "As a proof that many persons have survived after being scalped, we can assure our readers, that four

Highlanders are lately arrived from America, in order for admission into Chelsea Hospital, who had been scalped and left for dead."

Warren Johnson wrote in his journal on April 12, 1761 that, "there are many instances of both men and women recovering after being scalped." He also confirmed scalps were pulled "off from the back of the head."

The *New York Mercury* reported that about June 8, 1759, "two of our battoes were attacked on their way up the Mohawk's River, by a party of the enemy. The same party a day or two after scalped a woman, and carried off a child and a servant that were in company, between Fort Johnson and Schenectady; the woman lived 'til she got into Schenectady, tho' in great agony."

French-allied Native Americans skulked about British forts to inflict what casualties they could. Stephen Cross, a shipbuilder from Massachusetts, recorded the following on May 25, 1756:

> one of our soldiers came in from the edge of the woods, where it seems he had lain all night having been out on the evening party the day before and got drunk and could not get in, and not being missed, but on seeing him found he had lost his scalp, but he could not tell how nor when, having no others around. We supposed the Indians had stumbled over him in the dark, and supposed him dead, and taken off his scalp.

2. Early Settlers, Revolutionary War

Conflict between Native Americans and white settlers escalated during the last two decades of the eighteenth century. War—declared and undeclared—made for "dark and gloomy days," according to historian John F. Meginness in his *History of Lycoming County*. While frontier families of the West Branch Valley were "begging for help to protect them from the savages," Meginness writes, the Supreme Executive Council of Pennsylvania was asking counties to furnish additional men to serve with the Continental Army under General George Washington. There were few settlers in the region to respond to the call, however, since it had only been seven years since the land had been purchased from the Six Nations at the Treaty of Fort Stanwix.

The prominent Native American trails were the Susquehanna Path (also called Shamokin and Cinclacomoose), the primary method of travel from the east, and the Sheshequin Trail, which crossed the river at the head of Canfield Island and served as the chief thoroughfare north and south.

Because of Washington's maneuvers in New Jersey, New York, and eastern Pennsylvania, many settlers relocated to the state's interior. American settlers, though newly independent, struggled with the British monarchy, and the Indians struggled with the increasing tide of immigrating humanity, always encroaching despite land agreements.

"No one can blame the Indians for fighting to preserve their country," writes historian Paul A.W. Wallace in *Indians in Pennsylvania* (1961). "At the same time, it is difficult to blame the settlers, caught up as they were in one of the great mass movements of mankind. That does not mean that we must condone the crimes committed by those who cheated and murdered to gain their ends. It means only that we should not be unfeeling toward either side as we look back on the clash of the races. . . . "

The Battle of the Loyalsock

The Battle of the Loyalsock began with the ambush of settlers by a Native American war party that had slipped into the Loyalsock area by way of the

Sinnemahoning Path. A friendly Indian preceded the war party to warn the settlers and was ironically killed by a soldier at Fort Reed (now Lock Haven). His warning went unheeded.

A Captain Berry, who had been quartering at Samuel Wallis's home in Muncy, organized a dozen men to search for horses stolen by the Native-American war party. The soldiers followed the tracks to the Loyalsock and up past the narrows. Berry was warned several times to return to the Wallis homestead, but chose to ignore the reports. As the search party neared the narrows (present-day Four Mile Drive) on June 10, 1778, they were ambushed and most were shot. Four were taken prisoner, including an African-American slave who was later burnt at the stake.

Alarmed settlers fled to the safety of the Wallis homestead, but one farmer, John Thompson, decided to return home and retrieve his livestock. The Thompson farm was located along the Loyalsock Creek, near the site of the Berry massacre. Accompanied by Peter Shulfelt and 16-year-old William Wychoff, Thompson was ambushed by an Indian war party hidden in his barn. Thompson and Shufelt were killed. Wychoff was wounded and taken prisoner, but eventually recovered and was released.

After Thompson's death, his widow Juda resolved to leave the wilderness with her four-year old son. The epic journey of Juda Thompson, as described by Williamsport historian and archaeologist James Bressler, was prompted by her dire stress, despite the hardships and danger:

> Somehow she managed to find her way to Fort Augusta pulling a crude little cart in which she placed the little boy and a few items of clothing and the precious family Bible to sustain her. From thence, through storm, sunshine, dangers of the wilderness trail and savage adversaries, across streams and over mountains she pulled the little cart with its precious cargo 250 miles to her former home in New Jersey by way of Easton.

Her son, John Thompson Jr., became a prominent judge of Hunterdon County and raised a large family.

Another locally famous story is that of the Brady family and its enemy Chief Bald Eagle of the Wolf Clan of Delawares. According to C. Hale Sipe in *The Indian Chiefs of Pennsylvania* (1927), Bald Eagle "espoused the British cause, and his war parties brought death and desolation to the settlements on the West Branch of the Susquehanna."

Historians attribute the death of James Brady to Bald Eagle, and that of his father Captain John Brady to unidentified Iroquois. In vengeance, Bald Eagle was killed by the captain's surviving son, Samuel, the "most noted scout connected with Fort Pitt during the Revolutionary War," according to Sipe.

On August 8, 1778, James Brady and four militiamen were ordered to protect a group of settlers cutting a crop about 2 miles above Loyalsock. The crop belonged

A couple living in the rural area in the woods of Northcentral Pennsylvania during the pioneering days was not far removed from the lifestyle of the first settlers in Lycoming County. (JVBL.)

to Peter Smith on Turkey Run, "the unfortunate man that had his wife and four children murdered about a month previous," historians recount. Sentinels were placed at the opposite ends of the field, and the greater part of the grain was cut. The next day, the band returned to the field to finish its work. Under cover of an early-morning fog, Native Americans surprised the harvesters. A brief battle ensued; James Brady was attacked and fell.

"He was so stunned with the blow of the tomahawk, that he remained powerless, but strange as it may seem, retained his senses," writes Sipe. "They ruthlessly tore the scalp from his head as he lay in apparent death; and it was a glorious trophy for them, for he had long and remarkably red hair."

Men cradling grain in a nearby field came to assist and the Native Americans retreated. Meanwhile, James Brady, although scalped and wounded, crept to a cabin where Jerome Van Ness cooked for the soldiers and field workers. Van Ness attended to Brady's wounds then mustered help from nearby Fort Muncy. The soldiers took the young man home to his mother who "had a presentiment of something that was to happen, and being awake to alarms, met them at the river and assisted to convey her wounded son to the house," Sipe writes. "He presented a frightful spectacle, and the meeting of mother and son is described to have been heart-rending. Her heart was wrung with the keenest anguish, and her lamentations were terrible to be heard."

He lived five days and was delirious for the first four. On the fifth, his reason returned and he vividly described the attack. He said the Native Americans were of the Seneca tribe, and amongst them were Chief Cornplanter and Chief Bald Eagle.

Samuel hurried home to see his brother, but was too late, swearing vengeance on Bald Eagle and making "a solemn vow that he would never make peace with the Indians of any tribe." Nine months later, Captain John Brady was shot dead off his horse by three Native Americans secreted in a thicket, according to Sipe. His body was buried in an old graveyard near Halls, where a heavy granite marker was erected, bearing the following inscription:

Captain John Brady
Fell in Defense of Our Forefathers at Wolf Run
April 11, 1779
Aged forty-six years

Samuel, a ranger at Fort Pitt, renewed his vow of vengeance on all Indians—in particular on Chief Bald Eagle. He did not have long to wait. In June 1779, a band of the Wolf Clan of Delaware and probably some Seneca made a raid into Westmoreland County, attacking and killing settlers at James Perry's Mill. They also kidnapped several children.

Samuel Brady and a posse, painted and dressed like natives, ascended the Allegheny River looking for the culprits. He correctly suspected the Indians would be retreating to the north and staked out their camp, waiting for daybreak. "They attacked as the first streaks of dawn floated over the verdant hills of the Allegheny," Sipe writes, " . . . a sheet of flame blazed from the rifles of Brady and his men, and the chief of the seven Indians fell dead, while the others fled into the surrounding forest." Historians claim it was Brady's own rifle that brought down the Indian chief Bald Eagle. Sipe concludes:

> With a shout of triumph, Brady leaped upon the fallen chieftain and scalped him. Thus, on the banks of the Allegheny, far from the harvest field near the banks of the Susquehanna where Bald Eagle killed young James Brady during the preceding summer, Captain Samuel Brady avenged the death of his youngest and favorite brother.

The children were returned to the fort, and news of Bald Eagle's death led the Native Americans to refrain from more raids into Westmoreland that summer, according to Sipe. Samuel Brady continued to hunt and kill Indians until his death many years later in West Virginia.

SAMUEL WALLIS AND THE GREAT RUNAWAY

Another giant among early Lycoming County history was Samuel Wallis, probably the largest landholder in the area during the eighteenth century. According to

Meginness, Wallis was "the most energetic, ambitious, persistent, and untiring land speculator who ever lived in Lycoming County. His energy was marvelous, and his desire to acquire land became a mania which followed him to the close of his life." Among those great holdings, Wallis used 7,000 acres near Muncy to locate his estate anchored by a solidly built stone mansion, constructed in 1769 on the high ground near the mouth of Carpenter's Run.

"The location was well chosen," Meginness observed. "A few hundred yards north of the house Fort Muncy was afterward erected and became a rallying point for the settlers. Their home became a haven of rest for weary travelers. . . . They dispensed a liberal and elegant hospitality for the rude times in which they lived."

The homestead played a key role in the "Great Runaway." In the summer of 1778, following a series of Indian raids in the Susquehanna Valley above Shamokin, a captured Native American revealed that war parties planned to murder the settlers along both branches of the Susquehanna River. In a panic, people living above Lycoming Creek fled to Antes Fort. Those at the mouth of Bald Eagle Creek went to Harris Fort. People at Muncy were sheltered by Captain John Brady, and those settlers located from above Muncy to Lycoming Creek sought refuge at Wallis's, whose formidable homestead was one of the few structures in the Susquehanna Valley spared the Native Americans' torch.

The Indian war parties were urged, in part, by British officials as a way of opening a second front in their fight to put down America's independence aims. According to historian Carl Van Doren's book *The Secret History of the American Revolution*, published in 1941, Wallis might have played a large part in one of the most notorious cases of perfidy in American history.

Van Doren claims Wallis acted as an intermediary in transferring money between British General Sir Henry Clinton and American General Benedict Arnold in a treasonous plot to turn over the fort at West Point, New York, to the British. "There can be no doubt that Wallis was Arnold's agent and sent secret intelligence to the British," Van Doren wrote, "neither can there be that he had no scruple about making any money he could of shipping the British army of occupation food with which to carry on the war."

Other historians have cited Wallis's intrigues with the British. John Bakeless, in his 1959 book *Turncoats, Traitors and Heroes*, wrote, "Early in the war, [Wallis] had been, in some unknown way, extremely useful to the then British Commander in Chief General William Howe." He claims Wallis spied for the British on the movements of American General John Sullivan's expedition to relieve northern Pennsylvania and the southern tier of New York state of the Indian and British threat. Wallis arranged for a friend to volunteer for Sullivan's army as a secret informant and send reports that Wallis could pass on to his friend Major John Andre. Andre then could pass reports on to General Henry Clinton. Andre was hanged in the Arnold conspiracy and Arnold escaped to British lines, but nothing supposedly ever came of Wallis's plot.

Wallis also is alleged to have conspired to undermine the Sullivan Expedition. Noted for his knowledge of the "Indian Country," Wallis made available a falsified map to sabotage Sullivan's efforts, but Sullivan assembled navigational information from other sources and never used Wallis's bogus map.

Another alleged plot in which Wallis was ensnared, according to Bakeless, was a plan to use his home as an intelligence center for communications with noted Mohawk Chief Joseph Brant. The plan was to sow disorder among the Mohawk, who then would raid white settlements as a counter to the Sullivan Expedition. Nothing ever came of that plan either.

Despite all of Wallis's alleged machinations with the British, nothing prevented him from being appointed captain of the 6th Company, 2nd Battalion of the Northumberland County Associated Militia. Wallis also represented Northumberland County in the Pennsylvania Assembly in 1776.

After the Revolutionary War, in 1795, Lycoming County was created and Governor Thomas Mifflin appointed Wallis as one of the first four associate judges in the county judiciary. Wallis continued his land speculations, owning 300 acres near Grafius Run that he sold to Michael Ross for 5 shillings. Part of that land became Williamsport.

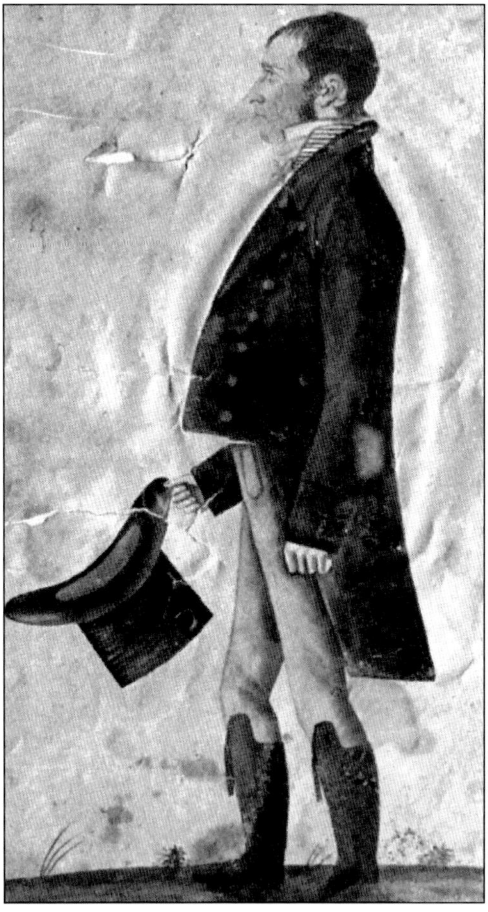

Michael Ross, founder of Williamsport, bought 285 acres of land from William Winter in 1793. It was that tract of land that later became present-day downtown Williamsport. (JVBL.)

Wallis served as a land agent for the Holland Land Company, a group of Dutch capitalists that also advanced large sums of money to Robert Morris, one of the major financiers of the American Revolution. The company was repaid with large tracts of land in Pennsylvania and New York.

Wallis worked with another agent for the Holland Land Company, James Wilson, a signer of the Declaration of Independence and one of the framers of the Constitution. Wilson later became an original member of the U.S. Supreme Court.

The financial dealings between Wilson and Wallis were quite extensive. As of May 1797, Wilson was indebted to Wallis for £88,500. Wallis often would use his beautiful plantation near Muncy as collateral in his many land dealings. When Wilson died in August 1798 without fully meeting his debt, it plunged Wallis into a serious fiscal crisis, but he would not live long enough to have to face it. He died in Philadelphia on October 14, 1798, reportedly of smallpox.

It has been said that all great men have feet of clay; Wallis is no exception. He seems to have had a dual quality: that of a great achiever and that of an infamous schemer, but it is unmistakable that he showed great humanity in granting refuge and comfort to those seeking safety from the Great Runaway.

PAUL REVERES OF THE WEST BRANCH VALLEY

While Washington's Continental Army fought the British, settlers along the Susquehanna River also considered themselves at war with the displaced Native Americans. Conflicts escalated daily, and rumors of a planned massacre of settlers were taken seriously. In August 1778, the Great Runaway began along the West Branch of the river and settlers fled from their homes with barely the clothes on their backs.

That so many settlers made it to safety has been credited to Rachel Silverthorn and Robert Covenhoven. Dubbed the "Paul Reveres of the West Branch Valley," both Silverthorn and Covenhoven rode horses throughout the valley warning settlers of impending Indian invasion.

Evacuating the countryside was not an easy task. Everything that could float was commandeered into service, including hastily constructed rafts. Women and girls manned the rafts, while men and boys walked the shores, driving cattle and warding off Native Americans. It was a tragic sight, eyewitnesses reported. One settler, Anna Jackson, recounted that all roads leading to the river were crowded with women and children fleeing the valley. "You may as well try to count the raindrops in a cloud as to try to count them," she said in an account reprinted in the Muncy Historical Society's quarterly publication *Now and Then* (1971).

The Great Runaway sent frightened convoys of settlers fleeing to Forts Muncy, Freeland, and Augusta as Native Americans sought vengeance throughout Northcentral Pennsylvania.

Silverthorn was an extraordinary woman, claims Katharine W. Bennet in the *Journal of the Lycoming County Historical Society* (Winter/Spring 1970–1971). "Many heroic women feature the frontier life of the state, but none excel in sheer bravery as Rachel Silverthorn," Bennet writes. "Mollie Pitcher operated a cannon at the battle of Monmouth, in place of her wounded husband, and Margaret Corbin, another Pennsylvanian, filled the place of her husband who had been killed at the siege of Fort Washington. But Rachel Silverthorn emulated Paul Revere. . . . Rachel's ride was to save her unsuspecting neighbors who lived along the half-beaten trail that followed Muncy Creek."

The Silverthorns were early settlers in Muncy Township and had been in Fort Muncy on August 8, 1778, when Continental soldiers, protecting farmer Peter Smith while he reaped his rye fields, were attacked by Native Americans. Among the soldiers was young James Brady, who was shot, wounded with a spear, and scalped by Chief Bald Eagle. Captain John Brady, father of James, was at the fort when the retreating soldiers brought news of the attack.

"Brave soldier that he was, he controlled his own anxiety and grief and thought of the safety of other harvesting bands that had gone from the fort that morning," Bennet writes. "He had the call of arms sounded and the little garrison was mustered on the parade ground in front of the fort."

The captain had his favorite horse saddled and asked, " 'Who will volunteer to carry the news of danger to our friends?' " Bennet reports.

No one stepped forward.

Brady raged, " 'This very night the wily varmints may creep up and when the first gleam of light shines over Muncy Hills, the scalping knife and tomahawks will again be flourished over their defenseless heads.' " The grief-stricken Brady thundered, " 'Who will go on this errand of mercy?' "

"A gentle voice on his right" volunteered. " 'I, Captain, I will tell them of their danger. I know the trails full well; I can make the circuit of the Gortners, John Alwood, the Shaners, David Aspen and the Robbs,' " Bennet writes. "And suiting the action to the word, Rachel Silverthorn sprang into the saddle and, before the soldiers had time to recover from their astonishment and chagrin, was flying with the speed of the wind toward the nearest cabin on the creek. Her timely warning was heeded, for under the cover of the dark night that followed, every exposed settler was safely housed in the fort. As for the brave Rachel, her return from the perilous mission was made as the captain predicted, before the last rays of sun vanished behind the Bald Eagle."

After Indian troubles depopulated the valley, the Silverthorn family made an early return, erected a temporary shelter on the charred remains of their log cabin, and made an effort to harvest their ripening grain fields.

Covenhoven was a highly regarded scout, spy, and guide. He was born "of Low Dutch parents in Monmouth County, New Jersey. He was much employed during his youth as a hunter and axeman to surveyors of land in the valleys tributary to the North and West Branches of the Susquehanna," writes Carlton E. Fink Sr. in the *Journal of the Lycoming County Historical Society* (Summer 1967).

He knew all of the paths in the wilderness, an attribute that made him useful as a scout and guide during the revolution. Covenhoven, Fink writes, "was fearless and intrepid, he was skillful in the wiles of Indian warfare and he

This house was built by Samuel Wallis in 1769 and is the oldest house in Lycoming County. During the Big Runaway, alarmed settlers fled to the safety of the Wallis homestead. (JVBL.)

possessed an iron constitution." He joined the campaigns under Washington and fought at the Battles of Trenton and Princeton. In the spring of 1776, Covenhoven returned home "where his services were more needed by the defenseless frontier," Fink writes.

By the spring of 1778, settlers were ordered to evacuate Fort Muncy and to seek refuge in Sunbury. No one would volunteer to carry the message to Fort Muncy except "Covenhoven and a young Yankee millwright," Fink continues. Reports were occasionally made of Covenhoven skirmishing with Native Americans, but after hostilities ceased, "our hero dropped from public view. His efforts in behalf of his neighbors were Herculean, when the emergencies demanded courage and skill; but as soon as the necessity for him had passed he modestly retired into oblivion, and never sought, at the hands of those he had so faithfully served, any recognition of his services."

His great-grandson, W.H. Sanderson, writes in the *Journal of the Lycoming County Historical Society* (Spring 1969) of his first meeting with Covenhoven. Sanderson recalls the man as being tall with long, gray hair streaked with red.

> He wore his hair straight down and combed it back over his ears. His eyes were brown and he had a florid complexion and a prominent nose. I was a little shy of him, as my mother had told me he was a great Indian Killer. But, after being around him for four or five days, I soon became very fond of him, as he was like an old soldier who always wanted to talk.

Sanderson remembers Covenhoven's black hunting knife. "On the back of this knife were filed 12 or 13 notches, and each notch represented an Indian killed by him. The gun used by Covenhoven was an old flintlock, with a barrel six feet long. I asked if the gun ever misfired, and he told me, 'Never when it was needed.' " The kind old man was interesting, Sanderson writes, "and he and I sat by the hour over the high banks of the river talking about his many adventures." Covenhoven died in October 1846 at the age of 90 and was buried in Northumberland.

CATHERINE SMITH: "CHILD OF SORROW"

While Michael Ross was settling the City of Williamsport, selling parcels of land to frontier families and immigrants, another enterprising resident of the West Branch Valley was being hoodwinked from her home and business. Catherine Smith, an old woman "of great business tact and energy," had erected gristmills and sawmills on White Deer Creek.

According to Meginness, Smith "was a child of sorrow and affliction." She was left a widow with ten children and no visible means to support her family except for 300 acres of forested land, which included the mouth of White Deer Creek. "There was a good mill seat at this point, and as a grist and saw mill were much wanted, she was often solicited to erect them," Meginness writes. The mills, completed in 1774 and 1775, "were of great advantage to the county; and the following summer, she built a boring mill where great numbers of gun barrels were bored for service in the Revolutionary army."

The widow Catherine Smith owned a grist and saw mill, similar to this early twentieth-century version in Muncy. Smith was a patriot during the Revolutionary War and converted her mill into a rifle manufacturing plant. (JVBL.)

Smith is considered a patriot because of her rifle-boring business and because she lost a son—"her greatest help"—during the conflicts. In 1779, marauding Native Americans burned her mills. Katharine W. Bennet, in her "Stories of the West Branch Valley," writes that Smith "returned to view the ruins wrought by war. The pioneers urged her to rebuild the grist and saw mills."

After much difficulty, she raised the money needed and, in 1783, rebuilt them. Before her business was underway, however, the firm of Claypool and Morris claimed a prior right to the land and brought ejection notice against her. "As frequently happened," Bennet writes, "the land office had given several warrants for the same tract, and the Claypool and Morris patent bore the earlier date."

Prominent residents and soldiers interceded on her behalf, and the widow walked to Philadelphia and back 13 times—in her bare feet—to plead her case. Dr. Lewis E. Theiss, in a 1950 speech to the Muncy Historical Society, discussed Smith's troubles:

> As I gather from other sources, the lawyers repeatedly double-crossed her. A hearing would be set for a given date. The troubled widow would take off her shoes and walk the 170 or so miles to Philadelphia in her bare feet. She could not afford to wear out her shoes—probably she had but one pair. She put them on at the last minute. The pioneers habitually went to church in the same way. When she got to court, the case had been postponed. There was nothing to do but trudge back home—barefooted.
>
> . . . there was a lot of fraud about land sales then. Indeed, when Ole Bull purchased the land for his colony of Norwegians up in the Coudersport region, well into the 19th century, he was defrauded and lost the entire tract of land, just as Catherine Smith lost her land.

No compromise was reached and, according to Bennet, "In spite of the justice of her claims and the efforts of her friends, the case was decided against her. In 1801, she gave up possession of the property that she had labored so hard to improve."

She might have retained her property through other means, however, writes Colonel Henry W. Shoemaker in a column printed on October 26, 1934 in the *Williamsport Sun*:

> On one of her first trips to Philadelphia, she was accompanied by her beautiful daughter, Cassandra, who created a sensation when she entered Independence Hall. Of the same witching, dark-eyed type as her mother had been in her youth, with the proud coronet features, she was a head taller than the old lady. She won the hearts of the susceptible legislators. It was asserted that one of the Claypool, a man of 45, wished to become the husband of Cassandra Smith. For this, he would quash the firm's claims and restore the property.

> . . . The lonely 22-year-old girl was willing to marry him, in order to see her mother made happy. But the stern old Roman matron refused this patrician alliance for her daughter and the return of her property by any "left-handed bargain," as she called it, and continued to fight her petition on to its final inglorious end.

Widow Smith died in poverty and was buried in the ancient settler's graveyard at the corner of Daniel Caldwell's barn. In making improvements years later, the farmer leveled the graveyard with the plow. Smith's bones were disturbed and those who knew her well recognized her skull—on account of its protruding teeth.

"There is something unspeakably pathetic in the history of this woman," Meginness concludes. "Her struggles in widowhood; what she accomplished for the benefit of early settlers; the fact that she furnished a mill for the manufacture of gun barrels to aid in the achievement of our liberties; her misfortunes and her last appeal to the law-making power for assistance; her death, burial and the final disturbance of her bones, afford a theme for a volume."

In recognition of her heroism, according to Shoemaker, a state commission selected a natural memorial to the Widow Smith and named the "noble culmination of Nittany Mountain, which looks down on the spot where she passed her most eventful and memorable days, 'Catherine's Crown.' " For her "relentless pursuit of righteousness, her lofty ideals and heroic efforts in the cause of freedom," and "though she was poor and obscure and had few educational advantages . . . she deserves a place among the seats of the mighty, right beside the greatest women of the land."

3. Organization of Lycoming County, Founding of Williamsport

American history is filled with rags-to-riches stories of great achievers and great personages, and local history is no exception. Michael Ross, the founder of the City of Williamsport, is one of those people. Ross was born on July 12, 1759 of Scottish origin. He and his mother came to Philadelphia about 1772, and the two became indentured servants to land speculator Samuel Wallis. Wallis brought them to his estate near Muncy.

During his servitude, Ross became a surveyor's assistant, a skill that would serve him well. He must have made a favorable impression on Wallis during his period of servitude because, at the conclusion of it in 1779, Wallis gave him a favorable recommendation and 109 acres of land. Ross became a successful surveyor and farmed on a large scale. He acquired various tracts of land and added to his acquisitions until he owned plots on both sides of the West Branch of the Susquehanna River.

In 1793, Ross bought 285 acres of land from William Winter. It was that tract of land that later became present-day downtown Williamsport. John Meginness writes in his *History of Lycoming County*, "The original plot of land was a rectangular figure containing 111 acres and divided into 302 lots with streets and alleys crossing each other at right angles."

Ross set aside some of the plots for use, such as a courthouse and jail, at the behest of William Hepburn, a strategic step in the decision to locate the county seat in the newly created Lycoming County in 1796. Thomas Lloyd's *History of Lycoming County* notes that Ross sold the first lots in what would become Williamsport on July 4, 1796.

On the western side of Lycoming Creek, within the southern part of the present boundaries of Newberry, was the area known as "Jaysburg," named for U.S. Supreme Court Chief Justice John Jay. The leaders of that community believed the new county seat should be there because it was the closest thing to a village west of Muncy. Another community, Dunnstown, located within the confines of the present-day Clinton County, also vied for the county seat. Williamsport ultimately would gain the honor through a combination of political influence and trickery.

State Senator William Hepburn, later to be the first president judge of Lycoming County, was a large landowner in the territory that became Williamsport, having great personal interest in seeing that Williamsport became the county seat. He joined forces with Ross by bringing all of his considerable influence to bear on the commissioners who would make the selection. There were even whisperings of bribery. The prominent men of Jaysburg did not sit idly by.

According to Meginness, the Jaysburg representatives claimed that their town was more suitably located on higher ground. They went as far as sending a messenger to Northumberland to obtain an affidavit from a man who would assert that Williamsport was a lowland area prone to flooding, an assertion proved by history.

The Hepburn-Ross group was alarmed by the potential harm that the affidavit would produce. When the messenger who obtained the affidavit returned, he stopped at the Russell Inn, which stood at the corner of present-day East Third and Mulberry Streets. There, he was plied with liquor and his saddlebags were stolen, along with the affidavit. The damaging information never reached the commissioners and Williamsport became the county seat.

Ross figures prominently in the naming of Williamsport. Various contentions have been made about the origin of the name, and some assert that it was named for William Hepburn. Others contend it was named for a surveyor friend of Ross by the name of Joseph Williams.

A more valid claim is that Ross named the town for his beloved son William. In April 1976, a Ross descendent, Mabelle J. Schuster of Orange, New Jersey, presented a leather-bound diary to the Lycoming County Historical Society. The book contains a page with the entry, "I name the borough of Williamsport for my son William, born on Jan. 22, 1795."

Ross died June 20, 1819. He was buried at the Pine Street cemetery, at the present site of the old city hall, and was later re-interred at the Williamsport Cemetery on Washington Boulevard.

William Hepburn: Father of Lycoming County

If Ross is noted as the founder of Williamsport, Hepburn can be regarded as the "Father of Lycoming County," as firmly a part of the genesis of the county as Ross is of the city.

Hepburn was born in Donegal, Ireland, in 1753 and came to America in 1773 or 1774. He lived for a time at Sunbury and came upriver to dig a race for Andrew Culbertson's saw and gristmill near present-day DuBoistown. A short time later, because of trouble with the Native-American population of the area, Hepburn became a member of the local militia. He rose through the ranks rapidly, becoming a colonel, and was commander of Fort Muncy at the time of the Great

William Hepburn, often called the Founder of Lycoming County, was a member of the local militia during the Revolutionary War. He rose through the ranks rapidly, became a colonel, and was commander of Fort Muncy at the time of the "Great Runaway" in 1778. (JVBL.)

Runaway in 1778. Hepburn ordered Robert Covenhoven to warn the settlers at Antes Fort and Fort Horn near Lock Haven. He married Crecy Covenhoven, Robert's sister, in the summer of 1777, and she bore him ten children.

Following the American Revolution, Hepburn bought a tract of 300 acres known as "Deer Park" within the limits of present-day Williamsport. He became a farmer, a distiller, a merchant, and later a justice of the peace. He was a generous man, as noted in the *Lycoming Gazette* of July 3, 1821, on the occasion of his death. After John Bennett and his bride paddled his canoe 6 miles downstream to have Hepburn perform the wedding ceremony, "the groom hesitantly informed him that he did not have enough money to pay the fee and buy a few articles necessary for housekeeping. Hepburn was so impressed with the frankness and honest appearance of Mr. Bennett that he not only remitted the fee but supplied him with some provisions from his store."

Hepburn was elected state senator representing Luzerne, Mifflin, and Northumberland Counties in January 1794. During his senate tenure, he played a critical role in the creation of Lycoming County, which was to be carved from territory taken from Northumberland County.

Hepburn received recognition for his military service and prowess in 1807, when Governor Thomas McKean appointed him a Major General of the 10th Division of the State Militia. He was prominent in church and fraternal affairs and was one of the early church fathers of Lycoming Presbyterian Church. He was instrumental in the founding of the first Masonic lodge in Lycoming County, a fraternity whose brethren long would be influential in the county's economic and civic life, and was elected the first Worshipful Master of Lodge 106, Free and Accepted Masons.

Hepburn's first wife died in 1800. He remarried shortly thereafter to Elizabeth Huston, who bore him nine more children. He died on June 25, 1821 at the age of 68.

FIRST ORDER: A COURTHOUSE, A JAIL

One of the first orders of business for county commissioners after establishing Lycoming County was the building of a courthouse and jail, the two facilities that placed the new county among the ranks of the "civilized and progressive" older counties.

County courts transacted business in a variety of temporary locations, including the Caldwell Tavern in Jaysburg (present-day Newberry); the public house of Eleanor Winter, located at the corner of the present West Fourth and Rose Streets; Thomas Huston's Rising Sun Tavern; and the Russell Inn located at the corner of Third and Mulberry Streets.

The first mention in the commissioners' minutes regarding a permanent courthouse appears on December 5, 1800, in which they authorized "the procuring

The Park Street mansion of Associate Judge William Hepburn was the second brick house in Williamsport. (JVBL.)

of a plan and draft of the Harrisburg courthouse." The first payment for material for the courthouse's construction was $16 to Thomas Harris on February 6, 1801. One unusual authorization for the construction of the courthouse was $6 to Jacob Grafius for "nine gallons of whiskey for the raising of the courthouse and offices." Apparently some of the men who constructed the courthouse were paid with whiskey and drank some of their "pay" while on the job. The courthouse was built on lots owned by Ross and was completed in 1802 for $20,417 by contractors John Turk and Edward Gobinn. John Burrows brought a bell from Philadelphia to place in the tower of the proud new building, made of bricks from the Hepburn's brickyard. The original courthouse lasted 60 years.

A new courthouse was built in 1860 and served the county well for more than 100 years. That structure was razed in 1969 and the present-day edifice built.

Work on the first jail started in December 1799 and was completed in 1801 at a cost of about $8,000, according to Meginness. A 20-foot wall faced William Street, and another faced Third Street, surrounding a two-story building.

In the front of the prison were rooms where some of the early Lycoming County sheriffs lived. One child of Sheriff Thomas Hays was born within the confines of the prison in 1822. The original structure was destroyed by fire in 1867 and was rebuilt at the same location, remaining in use as a prison until the 1980s. Still standing, its most recent incarnation is that of a restaurant and tavern.

Lycoming County: A Sum of Its Parts

In addition to Williamsport, Lycoming County consists of a number of important municipalities. The Borough of Jersey Shore resulted from territory taken from six land surveys in 1785. The first settler in what is now Jersey Shore was Reuben Manning, who located his home on a tract of land owned by his nephew Thomas Forster. Manning and Forster were both from Essex County, New Jersey. As the settlement grew, it became known as "Jersey Shore," a name used derisively by early Irish settlers there, because of Manning's and Forster's New Jersey origins. In 1805, the area was called "Waynesburg," but it never stuck. When the settlement was incorporated as a borough on March 15, 1826, the incorporation document read, "the place shall be called and styled the borough of Jersey Shore."

Several miles northeast of Jersey Shore, along the mouth of Larrys Creek, lies the borough of Salladasburg. Captain Jacob Sallade founded it in 1837 when he laid lots in the town and built Lutheran and Presbyterian churches. Sallade also built the first gristmill for the town. A tannery, owned by Robert McCullough, was the leading industry in the early years of Salladasburg. It was incorporated as a borough in 1884, with the slight difference in spelling.

Armstrong is the only township in Lycoming County that has had two boroughs carved from it. DuBoistown was the first of the two boroughs established. Located at the mouth of Mosquito Creek, it is on a tract of land once owned by Samuel Boone, brother of Hawkins Boone, a martyred Native-American fighter and cousin of the famous Daniel Boone. Andrew Culbertson owned 172 acres adjoining Boone's property, and established a gristmill, sawmill, and home for his family within the boundaries of present-day DuBoistown. In 1856, John DuBois purchased land within the boundaries of the area and laid out a town that he christened "DuBoistown." Thirty years later, he founded another town, this time in Clearfield County, which he just called "DuBois." DuBoistown was incorporated as a borough on October 14, 1878, despite opposition from residents of Armstrong Township.

The original settlers of the area that now is South Williamsport were Germans who settled near Hagerman's Run. The area around the Market Street Bridge once was known as "Rocktown" because of the rocky soil found there. Another section of present-day South Williamsport was called "Bootstown," named for a nearby man who stole a pair of boots.

Jacob Weise bought 40 acres within the boundaries of South Williamsport and laid it out in town lots, starting the area on the road to an organized town, as the South Williamsport Land Company was organized. Again, with some opposition from citizens from Armstrong Township, South Williamsport was incorporated as a borough on November 29, 1886.

According to John F. Meginness's *History of Lycoming County*, the first white man to settle in the area that became Hughesville was David Aspen in 1777. He fled the next year during the Great Runaway. The land where present-day Hughesville is located was sold to John Heap on May 7, 1793, and he in turn sold it to Samuel Harrold, who conveyed it to his son John. Jeptha Hughes bought the land from Harrold on March 23, 1816, and he laid out a town and named it "Hughesburg"; it was later changed to "Hughesville." In July 1820, Hughes sold the entire plot of land to Daniel Harrold. Paul Willey opened the first tavern there in 1820 and the first post office was established in 1827. Hughesville was incorporated as a borough on April 23, 1852.

About 2.5 miles north of Hughesville lies the borough of Picture Rocks. Nearby, a ledge of rocks rises from the bank of the Big Muncy Creek to a height of more than 200 feet. The first settlers there found a number of Native American pictures painted on the rocks, but the pictures have long since disappeared, and nobody ever translated the hieroglyphics. Legend has it that the flat area below the rocks was once a favorite camping spot for the Monsey Indians. A.R. Sprout and Amos Burrows founded the town in the fall of 1848, and some of their descendants still live there. The first post office was established in Picture Rocks in 1861, and the borough was incorporated on September 27, 1875.

One story illustrates the determined character of the early residents of Picture Rocks. Churchgoers met in an old, dilapidated schoolhouse, and a circuit preacher once remarked to one of the members of the church that he "dreaded attempting to preach in that pig pen of a house with such low ceilings and the broken walls." So the people of Picture Rocks acquired a lot, and through their combined labor and material, they erected a sturdy church in just eight days, one that served them well for more than 25 years.

This photograph from the late 1860s is of the Russell Inn, located at the corner of East Third and Mulberry Streets. It was one of the first buildings in Williamsport, and some early sessions of the county court were held there. It burned during the "Great Fire of 1871." (JVBL.)

According to historian Meginness, "There is much bold and beautiful scenery in easy view of Montgomery," and it continues to be one of Montgomery's major assets. Cornelius Low was probably the first settler in 1778, with John Lawson and Nicholas Shaffer soon following him. A town grew slowly and a post office, "Black Hole" with Samuel Ranck as its first postmaster, was established on March 26, 1836. In 1853, Black Hole became "Clinton Mills" and in 1860 it became "Montgomery Station." The borough of Montgomery was built on land taken from Clinton Township, and Montgomery became a borough on March 27, 1887.

The area of Muncy was one the earliest places to be settled in the West Branch Valley, surveyed by John Penn in 1769. Four brothers, Silas, William, Benjamin, and Issac McCarty, settled the area in 1787 and bought lots. In 1797, Benjamin McCarty laid out the town that he named "Pennsborough." The town grew slowly and was just a sleepy little village, earning the nickname of "Hardscrable." The first post office was established in April 1801. Pennsborough was incorporated as a borough on March 15, 1826. On January 19, 1827, the name was changed to Muncy because many people thought that the previous name was "too flat and too long." The new name would be more in keeping with the historical nature of the place and also would help to perpetuate the name of the Native Americans who used to reside in the area. The name of "Muncy" is derived from the Monsey Indians, a tribe of Delaware living there. The Monsey were eventually driven out and settled in another area that was eventually named for them: Muncie, Indiana.

4. Transportation Through the Susquehanna Valley and the Canal Period

The transportation of goods, services, and people was a rough and inefficient undertaking in the Susquehanna Valley in the early 1800s. This would change with the advent of the West Branch Canal. Colonials envisioned the idea of canals as far back as the mid-eighteenth century, but the creation of a canal system was postponed because of the tribulations of the Revolutionary War and later the birth pangs of nationhood.

On March 1, 1806, Governor Thomas McKean signed a bill elevating the village of Williamsport to a borough. The former outpost boasted 60 taxable citizens and settlers generally arrived by Conestoga wagon. Freight was shipped by keel or ark boat up the Susquehanna, named a public highway by a legislative act in 1783.

Williamson Road, completed in 1796, was the first land route through Williamsport. Instigated by Charles Williamson, a land agent for a London syndicate, his proposed roadway was to connect Sunbury with Bath, New York, a route that paralleled the Iroquois path called the Sheshequin Trail. The conclusion of the Williamson Road in 1796 and the genesis of the Sunbury-Williamson stagecoach run in 1809 nurtured the town's expansion.

William Packer's Canal System

Land travel was fine, but more was required to turn Williamsport into a commercial center. The need for a reliable water route was emphasized when the *Codorus*, a 60-foot steamship, arrived in Williamsport on May 3, 1826. It was a milestone in the city's transportation history and one that helped influence lawmakers.

On February 26, 1826, the Pennsylvania General Assembly authorized the creation of a canal system, looking to duplicate the success of New York's Erie Canal. Construction began on the West Branch of the Susquehanna's section of the canal system in 1828.

When the canal's Main Line was completed in 1831, construction of the promised West Branch Line was all but abandoned. It was at this crucial point that William F. Packer, a reporter for the *Lycoming Gazette*, authored the famous "Address to the People of Philadelphia." During his speech, Packer criticized the city for its breach of faith in failing to build the West Branch Canal. The Philadelphia Assemblymen responded by appropriating the funds, and Packer, then 25, was named superintendent of the new West Branch Division. It wasn't long before the ambitious young man was appointed commissioner of the entire canal system, then state auditor general. Elected to the Assembly in 1847, Packer became Speaker of the House and later governor of Pennsylvania. As the enterprise's formal champion, Packer enabled the canal to formally open on July 4, 1834.

The canal, at that time, only reached the mouth of Loyalsock Creek, and the first packet boat to navigate it was the *James Madison*. A group of local dignitaries, including former Governor J. Andrew Shulze, originally from Montoursville, rode the boat from Northumberland to the end of the canal. They were met at the lock point by the Williamsport Guards, commanded by Captain John Grafius, as well as a company of the Lycoming Cavalry. They took stagecoaches for the 3-mile trip to Williamsport.

Two years later, in July 1836, the canal, built almost exclusively by Irish immigrant laborers, linked Williamsport with Philadelphia and Pittsburgh. Packer

William F. Packer was the only Williamsporter to serve as governor of the Commonwealth of Pennsylvania. (JVBL.)

estimated the cost of the 73-mile canal that extended from Northumberland to Williamsport to Lock Haven and finally to Bellefonte at $1,158,580. In July 1944, Paul Rickolt wrote in the journal of the Muncy Historical Society, "The canal was 28 feet wide on the bottom, 40 feet wide at the top, and 8 to 10 feet deep."

Meginness writes in his *History of Lycoming County* of the canal's importance: "For many years the canal was an important water highway and it gave impetus to business that was felt in commercial circles throughout Lycoming County."

Terry Rhian discusses the economic impact of the canal in a paper titled "Williamsport's Economic Development During the Canal Period 1828–1850":

> The canal resulted in the bringing of people of working age to Williamsport, hence, increasing the growth of the economy through the development of manufacturers and industries. The completion of the West Branch Canal was the first forward step in transportation and as result revolutionized the trade pattern of the valley.

The canal provided manufacturers with the ability to ship goods to various locales, and as a result, a variety of new industries located in the Williamsport area. Because the canal wharves were at the foot of Market Street, the town became a major crossroads of trade in the West Branch Valley. Rhian asserts that "without the West Branch Canal, Williamsport would have remained a backwater, wilderness village."

The canal not only enhanced the economic development of Williamsport, it ushered in a new way of life. From the early settlement to the construction of the

A canal boat pulled by a team of horses is ready to offload goods to send to market. The shipment of trade was the primary function of the canals like the West Branch Canal. (JVBL.)

canal, all of the items needed by the residents were produced in the home, the field, the gristmill, and the blacksmith shop. Large-scale manufacturing was non-existent because of the difficulty in transporting supplies in and goods out of the region. In 1838, the first large sawmill in the county was constructed and was so profitable that others followed.

For the pilots of the freight boats, navigating the Susquehanna was a combination of the wild frontier and the sea. Passengers were enchanted by the romance of the river that was reminiscent of the Mississippi. During the daylong and overnight canal boat trips from Williamsport to Harrisburg, young men and women danced on the moonlit upper decks, while mature crowds played cards in the lounge.

Traveling on the canal boats, however, wasn't a romantic journey for novelist Charles Dickens, who toured Pennsylvania while in America. "Crowded by the cramped quarters, nauseated by foul cigar smoke, and repelled by American expectorating habits, Dickens thought the most welcome part of the packet trip was the brisk walk that could be taken on the towpath before breakfast while the horse teams were being switched," writes James C. Humes in *Sweet Dream: Tales of a River City*.

Canal Riot of 1833

The competition between freight boats was fierce, and even though a 4-mile-per-hour limit had been set for the river, they often raced each other to the locks. Main Line canalmen would jeer their West Branch rivals singing, "West Branch drivers, They think they are so nice; They sit on the saddle mule and pick off the lice."

The songs and chants were "fighting words" for the canalmen, who often fought amongst themselves, with the lock tenders, construction crews along the route—even pirates. One of the most colorful events of the West Branch Canal was the Canal Riot of 1833. The 1830s was a decade that saw a great influx of foreign laborers, mostly Irish, to the area to help build the waterway. It also was a period of great anti-foreign agitation and resentment by the native-born of the area.

Laborers were not well treated by their employers. With inadequate wages, long hours, and substandard housing, they often were plied with liquor, keeping them drunk so that they would not complain of their poor lot. Tensions finally exploded on August 23, 1833, at Jane Hunt's orchard, near the Great Island Dam, Dunnstown, an area then a part of Lycoming County. (Clinton County was not created until 1839.)

An Irish worker on the canal was in the process of knocking fruit from trees in the Hunt orchard, when Hunt's son Jesse shot him, wounding the Irishman slightly before he fled. The native-born boatmen hauling stone for the canal taunted some of the Irish workers about the incident, and the Irish attacked the boatmen with picks, shovels, and spades. In the ensuing fray, one of the Irishmen was wounded by gunfire and stabbed.

The laborers returned to work the following day and cooler heads prevailed for a while. Then, when darkness fell, about 50 of the Irishmen gathered near the shanty of the job supervisor, severely beating the man and some of his friends, and attempted to tear down the building. They attacked native-born people in the area, destroying some structures, but wild rumors circulated about the extent of the troubles. The local militia was notified, and elements of the Lycoming Cavalry and a company of Centre County infantry responded.

Squire Joseph Parsons witnessed the event:

> At the break of day the next morning, the military were in line, and marched, with flags flying and the beat of drums, to the scene of the strife. When the insurgents saw them coming, they turned their faces to the hills and fled like foxes. They could not, armed only with their spades and picks, face the formidable militia. The effect of the appearance of the well-equipped column can easily be imagined.

Seventy of the Irish rioters were arrested, but only 16 were held over in the Lycoming County Jail for trial. After the tensions and excitement subsided, those arrested were given short jail sentences or light fines.

Unfortunately, in that time of poor communications, the extent of the riot was exaggerated as the story spread. In Williamsport, it had been rumored that more than 500 Irish rioters had been met by more than 250 militiamen, and that many were wounded in the clashes. The amount of property damage also had been exaggerated, but the violent clashes were symptomatic of a time of great intolerance to foreign people and their cultures.

RAILROAD SOUNDS DEATH KNELL OF CANAL SYSTEM

The canal eventually was superseded by the railroads as the primary means of transportation and the great flood of 1889 spelled the end of the West Branch Canal. Ironically, State Senator William Packer, once the region's strongest proponent for canal development, yielded to its strong rival, the railroad. In 1851, he sponsored a railway bill connecting Washington and Baltimore with the Great Lakes. As the pre–Civil War governor, he eventually officiated over the demise of Pennsylvania's waterway dominion.

The first railroad in the county ran from Williamsport to Ralston in 1839, but it wasn't until 1855 that the rails provided access to other markets. Lumber, coal, and iron-ore could be transported easily by rail, resulting in the development of large industries. Improved transportation brought an inflow of tradesmen and craftsmen as shops opened throughout the county, and steam mills supplanted the small grist and sawmills that had operated by overshot waterwheels. Soon the county boasted woolen mills, tanneries, foundries, machine shops, steel mills, furniture factories, and other industries that could produce products comparable to those made throughout the state.

The Industrial Revolution had arrived in Lycoming County.

5. The Lumber Boom

The need for finished lumber furnished the stimulus for the building of the region's first sawmills. The pit saw, a common crosscut rip saw with one person in a pit and another on top of the log furnishing the power, was the earliest device for manufacturing lumber in large quantities. It soon was replaced with the "up and down" saw, which was powered by water, then improved by the addition of "slabbers," flat or rolling gangs.

Roland Hall built the first sawmill in the county in 1792 on the banks of Lycoming Creek, 4 miles from the Susquehanna River. Although crude in its construction, it provided the lumber for many of the first houses in Williamsport. Six years later Samuel Torbett erected a mill on Bottle Run, and Thomas Caldwell attached a sawmill to his gristmill on the same creek.

Peter Tinsman introduced Williamsport's first steam sawmill on January 1, 1852. Circular saws were introduced at the steam mill, but there were two complaints: the kerf (width of the cut) made by the saw wasted lumber, and often it was not big enough to cut large logs. The band saw, an endless belt of flexible steel-saw that cuts logs of large diameter, improved the situation, and is used today in many large operations.

Lumbermen either bought the timberland or paid in fee simple. Many of them owned hundreds of acres of land that became useless when stripped of the trees. To avoid becoming "land poor" many bought only standing trees of a certain size, leaving the title to the soil and mineral rights to the original owner—a practice that hastened the denuding of the forests. A timber estimator would travel the tract of land and calculate the amount of lumber it could produce. Another method of purchase was by use of an expert "scaler," a person selected by the seller and buyer who estimated the number of log feet before payment was made.

Jobbers cut logs at an agreed price, then a crew of lumberjacks cut the trees into correct proportions and piled them on skidways or beside streams. Lumberjacks cut trees in two periods: fall and winter, and early spring through early summer. Hardwood trees, for the most part, were not peeled and could be cut in the fall and winter. Void of foliage, they were more economical to harvest. Hemlock trees could be peeled only from the early spring through late June because of the sap.

After logs had been cut, they had to be transported to sawmills. Heavy hardwoods and the lighter white pine and hemlock demanded different methods of movement. Only the lighter wood would float and was sent downstream as soon as the heavy ice cleared. Hardwoods such as oak and maple were conveyed on sleds.

Lumbermen often built splash dams to send the logs downstream. Only experienced men were trusted. Wearing heavy, high-topped shoes and thick woolen clothes, the drivers chased the logs and broke logjams with "picklevers" or "canthooks." Free-floating logs often created tangled masses, and the most experienced driver (sometimes called a jam cracker) had to locate the "key" log—the log that once released would disperse the pile—and free it. Sometimes the key log could not be budged and the drivers would use dynamite to break the jam.

The drivers followed the logs with teams of horses and often would have to drive the horses into the streams. On larger streams, driving crews used large ark rafts that served as portable bunkhouses, often sleeping in wet clothing.

The lumber sled was necessary to move heavy logs off of the mountain. Low-slung and narrow, the horse-drawn sled could negotiate mountain trails with large logs on the snow and ice. As the accessible forests were denuded, lumbermen had to move higher up the slopes, making it imperative to cut the lighter trees for floating down the streams.

Another method of moving logs was the slide. Log troughs were built and the insides were either oiled or iced. Logs would hurtle at top speed, sometimes flying off the slide. The logs would pile up at the bottom of the slide, so iron spikes were imbedded in the slide to slow them.

JAMES PERKINS AND HIS SUSQUEHANNA RIVER BOOM

One of the most important men of vision and entrepreneurial skill who helped to develop Williamsport and Lycoming County into a major center of commerce was Major James H. Perkins. His foresight and boldness helped to make Williamsport the "Lumber Capital of the World" in the mid- to late nineteenth century. In 1845, Perkins moved to Williamsport where he and his business partner, John Leighton, wished to engage in the lumber manufacturing business. He bought Williamsport's only sawmill, known as the "Big Water Mill."

Perkins envisioned Williamsport as the major center for the lumber industry because the area possessed a bountiful supply of timber and had the natural advantage of the Susquehanna River to float that timber to market. To fully exploit these advantages Perkins decided to create a "boom" to catch and secure the logs that came into the river so that they would not float away helter-skelter from the mills that were supposed to process them.

In 1849, Perkins, along with John Leighton, John Dubois Jr., Matthias Dubois, Issac Smith, and Elias S. Lowe, formed the Susquehanna Boom Company. The boom consisted of a chain of logs stretched diagonally across the river near the present-day Susquehanna State Park. Cribs caught the logs, and the boom

Major James H. Perkins, along with several other financiers, formed the Susquehanna Boom Company in the 1850s. It was the most important development in Williamsport, helping the town to become the "Lumber Capital of the World." (JVBL.)

stretched from Williamsport to Linden. The 6-mile stretch was able to hold 300 million feet of logs at one time.

At the height of the lumber era, 30 large sawmills operated in Williamsport. In 1873, the peak year, 1,582,450 logs were converted into lumber. Gladys Tozier, in an article in the *Journal of the Lycoming County Historical Society*, wrote that Perkins's construction of a boom "revolutionized the lumber industry and made Williamsport famous in all the lumbering industry and countries." Meginness amplified this, writing, "Williamsport owes its development and prosperity to the lumber manufacturing industry." The boom ushered in a period of lumber prosperity that would last for more than 40 years.

Perkins contributed another economic innovation to the area in the early 1850s when he started the practice of paying workers in cash. Up to this point, workmen were compensated in something that resembled a barter system, in which they were paid in "written exchanges" or "written orders." This system gave undue advantage to employers. The introduction of payment in cash by Perkins helped to make things more equitable for workers.

His financial pluck placed Perkins in the forefront of Williamsport's business class, and his financial wisdom placed him in a good position to help found one of Williamsport's first banks, the Savings Institution of Williamsport. He served as mayor of Williamsport from 1870 to 1872.

Loggers use mules to haul heavy logs out of the woods toward a sawmill for processing into lumber. (JVBL.)

LUMBER BOOM'S COLOSSUS: PETER HERDIC

Peter Herdic looms over Williamsport's "Lumber Boom Era" like a colossus. Herdic arguably has left a greater imprint on the posterity of Williamsport and Lycoming County than any other man. At 20, he worked at a sawmill and saved his hard-earned money, and in 1846, along with William Andress, opened a sawmill in Cogan House Township. He moved to Williamsport in 1853, a village of only 1,700 inhabitants at the time.

He bought a tract of timberland in 1854 and erected a steam sawmill, then sold the timber from his land for $10,000 and the sawmill for $1,200, reinvesting the proceeds into other timberlands and other speculative projects. During the next ten years, he purchased more land, built houses, sawmills, and other lumber-related industries, and helped to power the lumber prosperity that came to Williamsport in the 1850s and 1860s.

Herdic played a major role in the transportation infrastructure in the Williamsport area, using his political and monetary influence to persuade the Philadelphia & Erie Railroad to move its passenger depot from Pine Street to the area around present-day Park Home. This was not necessarily a philanthropic gesture on his part since he owned the land and stood to profit greatly from the move.

He was the driving force behind the founding of the Williamsport Passenger Railway Company, although the company was not very profitable under his leadership; he sold it 1879. He also invented a form of transportation that was the predecessor of the taxicab—a horse-drawn carriage with side seats and a back entrance. He was immortalized by having this form of transportation listed in some dictionaries as the "herdic."

Herdic was the leading force behind the development of what became "Millionaires Row." He owned property on a stretch of West Fourth Street and built several fine houses along it. Noted architect Eber Culver designed the houses for Herdic, with the most notable surviving edifice being Park Place, which began as the Herdic House hotel in 1865.

Several churches became the beneficiaries of Herdic's generosity. The most notable example was the Trinity Episcopal Church, built at his expense on property that he owned. He provided the property for the Annunciation Catholic Church, the Congregational Church, and the First Evangelical Lutheran Church. He also contributed generously to the building of the first Jewish synagogue in Williamsport, Temple Beth Ha Shalom.

Lumber workers move logs from a nearby stream to the Susquehanna using horses to steer the logs in the direction of the numerous mills in the Williamsport area. There the timber was processed into lumber. (JVBL.)

Herdic was instrumental in having Williamsport chartered as a city in 1866 by the state legislature. He was elected the city's mayor in 1869, and it is believed that it cost him $20,000 to get elected, often leaving $10 and $20 bills among the bottles of many saloonkeepers.

Control of the Susquehanna Boom Company in the 1860s helped line Herdic's pockets further. He used that control to levy high charges on lumbermen needing the boom to get their logs to market. These lumbermen sought relief from the state legislature, but Herdic's money and influence bought legislators' allegiance to his interests.

Herdic's big borrowing ways finally caught up to him during the Financial Panic of 1873. The hard times produced by this panic prompted Herdic to declare bankruptcy in 1878. But he rose from the financial ashes, becoming a leading force in the erection of waterworks at Selinsgrove and Huntingdon, Pennsylvania, and Cairo, Illinois. It was while at Huntingdon that Herdic slipped on the ice and fractured his skull, an injury resulting in his death on March 2, 1888.

LUMBER BARON MAHLON FISHER

A showplace of Williamsport's lumber boom era was the home of lumber baron Mahlon Fisher. At first a farmer, he learned the carpenter's trade, which led to an interest in architecture. He became one of Flemington's leading and innovative architects, designing many prominent and fine Greek Revival-style buildings there.

The lumber business beckoned and Fisher moved to Williamsport in 1855. He became a partner in two lumber firms and a planing mill, and later became

A lumber ark is a shack built on a raft in which men slept and ate during the lumber season. Horses were stabled on logging drives. This picture is from about 1900. (JVBL.)

president of the Susquehanna Boom Company. The financial community felt Fisher's influence in a major way as one of the organizers and directors of the old Lumbermen's National Bank and one of the original members of the Williamsport Land Company. Additionally, he was president of the Valentine Iron Works.

He also was a philanthropist, donating large sums of money to establish and maintain the First Baptist Church of Williamsport. He established a trust, the proceeds of which were used to help the widows and orphans of Williamsport.

Fisher wanted a residence that befitted his prominence in the community and commissioned noted architect Eber Culver to design it. A magnificent mansion that cost more than $1 million was erected at 815 West Fourth Street, the site of the present-day YWCA. The Fisher mansion was heated by steam and boasted two towers, a carriage house, an English garden, and a greenhouse.

The Fisher home was considered one of the focal points of Williamsport's high society in the late nineteenth century. It had high ceilings and a large reception hall with a rotunda. In a touch borrowed from the White House, the home contained a red room in the northeast corner and a blue room that served as the parlor. The walls were erected under the supervision of David Stuempfle, proprietor of the West Branch Stone Works. When the Fisher home was torn down in 1926, it was estimated that there were more than 250,000 bricks in it.

Eber Culver Builds Millionaires Row

The Herdic House, the Park- Home, Williamsport's first city hall, the Trinity Episcopal Church, the Weightman Block, and 13 mansions along Williamsport's "Millionaires Row" are among the many buildings that architect Eber Culver designed during the mid- and late nineteenth century. He left an enduring architectural legacy that continues to enrich the area.

Culver was born near Auburn, New York. At the age of 16, he became an apprentice to a carpenter in Dayton, Ohio, but he never had formal architectural training, regarding himself as a "practical builder." He arrived in Williamsport in 1855 and helped design some of the larger sawmills and planing mills that helped to service the lumber boom. For the next 40 years Culver enjoyed his greatest period of architectural design creativity. In 1863, he formed the Culver and Barber Company to promote building in the area. The company flourished, and in 1874, Peter Herdic enlisted Culver's talents as chief architect of his emerging empire.

He designed many of the buildings that Herdic became associated with, such as the Herdic Hotel, later known as the Park Home, Herdic's own home, the Trinity Episcopal Church, and what became the "Weightman Block." Herdic paid Culver $2,000 a year for his services.

The period from 1883 to 1894 was Culver's most productive period while in Williamsport. The buildings he designed during this period include the old Williamsport High School, other school buildings on Memorial Avenue and Penn Street, the old Williamsport City Hall, the Lycoming Opera House, the Susquehanna Trust and Safe Deposit Company, and the Hess Block.

Workers gather at the Sones sawmill at Masten during the lumbering era. Mills like this ringed the Greater Williamsport area, particularly near the Susquehanna River. (JVBL.)

WILLIAMSPORT'S FOREMOST CITIZEN

Forceful and resourceful, J. Henry Cochran has been described as Williamsport's foremost citizen. Cochran started a lumber mill at the foot of Park Street and then acquired John Reading's extensive holdings in the Susquehanna Boom Company. For many years, he was regarded as the leading lumberman in the area and was the last company president who helped to develop the timber wealth around Williamsport.

Following the great 1889 flood, Cochran diversified his financial interests, investing in the Wire Rope plant and the Lycoming Foundry and Machine Company. He helped to bring other industry to the city through his presidency of the Board of Trade, predecessor to the chamber of commerce.

Cochran was prominent in political circles and was the Democratic Party's kingpin in Lycoming County. He was elected to the state senate in 1894 and served there for 16 years, acting as minority leader for a time. His high political connections extended to President Grover Cleveland, with whom he had a close friendship—instrumental in dispensing his party's patronage in Pennsylvania. He also served as a delegate to three Democratic national conventions. He was offered the Democratic nomination for governor, but he declined. Generous in his support of charitable causes, many times he contributed anonymously. The area's transportation infrastructure received extensive financial attention from Cochran and he was a prominent member of all of the area's Masonic bodies.

THE SAWDUST WAR

America in the 1870s was rife with labor strife and turbulence. Lumber camps and sawmills of the Williamsport area were no exception. In 1872, Williamsport's lumber boom was in full flower and great fortunes were being made by a select few. The great wealth did not make its way to the workers whose labors made it possible. Lumber workers were poorly paid as they faced hazards, including injury or death without compensation.

It was against this backdrop that the Pennsylvania legislature passed a law (with no enforcement provisions) for an eight-hour day for workers in May 1868. In May 1872, the State Labor Reform Convention was held at the courthouse in Williamsport—a convention of labor organizations formed in 1871, serving as the impetus for the beginning of labor agitation among lumber workers. Local union organization began led by, among others, Thomas Greevy.

At a union meeting on June 26, 1872, the gathered workmen passed a resolution demanding a ten-hour workday. Several months before, the men who controlled the lumber trade formed the Lumbermen's Exchange, a cartel to control and monopolize lumber affairs. The Lumbermen's Exchange answered the union threat by refusing to negotiate with the workmen, and they retaliated. Mayor

Distinguished lumberman and politician J. Henry Cochran also founded the Williamsport Board of Trade, predecessor to the Chamber of Commerce. (JVBL.)

Starkweather of Williamsport dismissed one policeman, James S. Bermingham, because of his involvement with the union.

Union members went on strike, their slogan being "Ten Hours or No Sawdust," and they marched with banners and drums beating. Tension mounted, with the mayor and county sheriff calling on Governor James Geary to declare martial law and activate the state militia. He initially refused this request.

Labor leaders claimed that they were not on strike but were only seeking the rights due them. Negotiations continued and there were cracks in the Exchange's resolve. Peter Herdic and several other ownership members supported the ten-hour demand, but the Lumbermen's Exchange closed all of the mills, as well as the Susquehanna Boom.

On July 22, mill owners decided to open the mills, initiating a confrontation with the strikers. Troops finally were called out—eventually 500 of them—including two Williamsport militia companies: the Williamsport Greys, and the all-Black Taylor Guards, led by First Sergeant Jim Washington, a former slave. Militia companies marched on the angry crowd of strikers with fixed bayonets and the strikers dispersed. Strike leaders Thomas Greevy, A.J. Whitten, Thomas Blake, and James Bermingham were arrested, but newspaper accounts of the time were sympathetic to their plight. This would have a positive outcome for those arrested.

A painting, now in the Thomas Taber Museum of the Lycoming County Historical Society, depicts state militia moving against striking lumber mill workers during the "Sawdust War" of 1872. The workers were striking for a ten-hour day. (WSG/GRIT.)

A sign on a small boat proclaims the end of the Susquehanna Boom, the large boom in the Susquehanna River that helped to capture millions of logs. The boom operated from the 1840s until the early 1900s. (JVBL.)

There was a large protest meeting held at the courthouse on July 30, urging the release of the strike leaders, but to no avail. After a short trial that began on September 3, the men were found guilty and sentenced to one year of hard labor. On the day that their sentences were to begin, however, Governor Geary granted a full pardon, citing a petition for their release with more than 2,000 signatures. It is speculated that Peter Herdic, who supposedly had great influence with Geary, also was partly responsible for the pardon.

This first attempt to organize lumber workers failed and it would take until the early years of the twentieth century before any attempts at labor organizing in Lycoming County would be successful.

The lumber labor dispute in Williamsport foreshadowed the bloodier and more costly labor strife that erupted in the anthracite coal fields in northeastern Pennsylvania in the mid- and late 1870s, highlighted by the Molly Maguires and their attempts to gain economic justice for coal miners.

The lumber industry and its barons denuded the forests, then moved on, leaving thousands of timberless land upon which they were obliged to pay taxes. The Commonwealth of Pennsylvania bought most of it for back taxes and the state government set about reforesting the land. Forest trails and roads, as well fire observation towers, were constructed to help maintain the state-owned lands. For the purpose of reforestation, the state established its first tree nursery at Mount Alto. Today, the forests are protected as moderators of floods and droughts, places of recreation, and hunting preserves.

6. Abolition and the Underground Railroad

Abolition of slavery excited great passions throughout the United States during the pre–Civil War period and Lycoming County was no exception. This was amply demonstrated in a little-known incident known as the Abolition Riot of 1842.

It is usually assumed (incorrectly) that the people of the North were of one mind about the abolition of slavery, condemning it, and working hard for its elimination. The New England states were the hotbed for abolition, but people in states such as Pennsylvania were much more divided on the issue. Some were openly hostile to the doctrine of abolition and were at the center of the Riot of 1842.

Enos Hawley, a tanner by trade and later the postmaster of Muncy, hated the institution of slavery, owing to his Quaker heritage. He was not shy about his revulsion, and in the spring of 1842, Hawley invited a like-minded speaker to town. The unknown, itinerant abolitionist's appearance was not welcomed by all, as 18 men attacked the schoolhouse where the speaker was delivering an address, pelting the building with rocks and various other missiles, knocking out all of the windows, and causing some injury to the speaker and his sponsor. After Hawley and the speaker left the building, the men continued to pelt them with eggs. Even when the two reached Hawley's house, the rowdies continued to throw objects.

The roughnecks were indicted on charges of "riotously, and tumultuously assembly to disturb and disturbing the peace of the Commonwealth" in August 1842. They were placed on trial in September. The jury found 13 of the 18 guilty of the charges after much wrangling during the deliberations. One member of the jury, ardent abolitionist Abraham Updegraff, later wrote about his experience. He described a long and contentious process in which he had to use all of his persuasive powers. The initial jury ballot came in at eleven for acquittal and one against. Updegraff argued to the other jurors with "we have been sworn to try this case according to the law and the evidence presented and that if no contradictory evidence is offered by the defendants than we could nothing more but to convict them."

Updegraff used his knowledge of German to persuade three other jurors in their native tongue to see things his way. Another poll was taken, resulting in nine for conviction and three for acquittal. Finally, on the third try, the jury convicted them.

But the jury's decision was effectively annulled when Governor David Rittenhouse Porter pardoned the convicted defendants several days after the trial, making it clear that the incident had larger social and political implications, since governors rarely intervened in such cases. His pardon message said, in part, "It is represented to me by highly respected citizens of Lycoming County, that this prosecution was instituted more with a view to the accomplishment of political ends than to serve the cause of law and order." Porter's pardon message blamed the abolitionist speaker for the disorder stating that the content of the speech was "notoriously offensive to the minds of those to whom they were addressed and were calculated to bring about a breach of the peace."

As a result, Porter was given the derisive nickname of "The Pardoning Governor."

DANIEL HUGHES AND FREEDOM ROAD

The Underground Railroad ran from the American South through the northeastern states to Canada from the 1790s until the Civil War. Lycoming County, because of its strategic location, was one of the most important stops on the road to freedom for escaping slaves.

There were two main centers of Underground Railroad activity in Lycoming County: the Pennsdale-Muncy area with its large Quaker population, and an area just north of the city of Williamsport, where Daniel Hughes lived. Known at the time as "Nigger Hollow," the road was more appropriately renamed "Freedom Road," thanks to Hughes, one of the most courageous people in the story of the Underground Railroad.

Hughes was a part-Mohawk Indian born at Canasteo, New York, in 1812. He was a man of towering stature at over 6 feet, 7 inches, and weighed approximately 300 pounds. He moved to the Williamsport area in 1828 where he married Ann Rotch, an African-American woman.

Hughes's occupation as a lumber river raftsman operating on the Susquehanna River between Williamsport and the Baltimore area enabled him to smuggle escaped slaves to Williamsport, where he hid the fugitive slaves at his house in the woods. It was a natural haven, reinforced by a series of caves that were located on and near the Hughes property.

It took great courage and resourcefulness to "conduct" escaped slaves along the Underground Railroad. Hughes, his wife, and their 16 children exposed themselves to great risk in their quest to help the slaves "Follow the North Star to Freedom," or as an old Underground Railroad song stated, "Follow the Drinking Gourd." It was against the law to assist runaway slaves, punishable by imprisonment and fines. Also, many people in the area were unsympathetic to the runaways' plight, and the Hughes and others who aided them were subject to harassment and even physical violence.

The imposing Daniel Hughes, perhaps the Williamsport area's most famous conductor of the Underground Railroad during the period 1840 to 1861, risked his life, and his family's lives, to help runaway slaves. (WSG/GRIT.)

Hughes operated on moonless nights, avoiding the possibility of detection by slave catchers who became more prevalent after the passage of the Fugitive Slave Act of 1850. The act allowed catchers to operate in the northern states with no legal restrictions as they sought to bring escaped slaves back into bondage in the South. To thwart them, Hughes and his sons stretched horsehair from one side of trails to the other, hoping to knock the catchers from their horses and slow down or deter their pursuit.

Hughes and his son conducted runaways to the next station in Trout Run. After Trout Run, slaves fled to Elmira, New York, and eventually into Canada where they were not subject to arrest and a return to slavery. Hughes's son Robert reminisced as an old man:

> We would hide them in the woods in brush houses. I was just a little boy, but I remember very well carrying meals out to them in the woods. They usually traveled in groups of two or three men. Often patrollers would come to our place looking for runaways. They never caught anyone at our place. Rich people and good church people in Williamsport, mostly Quakers, helped in the work.

The Hugheses donated a portion of their land along Freedom Road as a cemetery for African Americans. Among those buried there are nine African-American veterans of the Civil War. A Pennsylvania Historical Marker stands at the site.

The account of Hughes and the other Lycoming Countians who participated in helping with the Underground Railroad is detailed in the documentary film "Follow the North Star to Freedom," made by area historian and documentary filmmaker Karen Frock. Assisting Frock in the film was the great-granddaughter of Daniel Hughes, Mamie Sweeting Diggs, who has spoken far and wide to preserve the legacy of her family's courageous contributions to the cause of liberty.

The Friends of Pennsdale

It is no accident that one of the main centers of the Underground Railroad in Lycoming County was the Pennsdale-Muncy area, where many members of the Society of Friends, or "Quakers," lived. In fact there still is a Quaker Meeting House there. Members of the Society of Friends were among the most ardent abolitionists and most active conductors of the Underground Railroad.

The Quakers of the Pennsdale-Muncy area probably were influenced in their abolitionist thinking by one of the Society of Friends's leading theologians, John Woolman (1710–1772). He abhorred slavery, preaching against its evils and urging fellow Quakers who were slaveholders to abandon the immoral practice. Woolman traveled extensively in the New Jersey-Pennsylvania region, and when he stayed with Quakers who held slaves, he made a practice of paying his host for slaves' services.

One of the most famous Underground Railroad stations in Lycoming County was in Pennsdale, and was known as the "House of Many Stairs." At the time of its service on the Underground Railroad, it was the Bulls Head Tavern owned by Edward Morris. It served as a stagecoach stop, offering food, drink, and lodging, so the busy comings and goings help to mask the sanctuary activities that the tavern offered for runaway slaves.

The House of Many Stairs was constructed of lime and fossil stone with a wooden roof, built on a hillside, resulting in an abundance of stairs that gave the house its nickname. The many steps helped to confuse any slave catchers who might be on the trail of runaway slaves. There were a number of hidden rooms that provided shelter, and a cubbyhole with a sliding panel at the head of one of the stairways also concealed the runaways.

Another Pennsdale sanctuary for escaped slaves was Wolf Run House owned by Quaker William Haines. Three generations of the Haines family were involved in Underground Railroad activities.

The Quaker Meeting House in Pennsdale served as an assembly point for the runaway slaves to continue their travels north along the Genesee Trail into New York and then into Canada. Conductors of the Underground Railroad encouraged a story that the area around the meeting house was haunted. Word circulated that strange, unearthly groans had been heard in the area of the graveyard of the meeting house late at night, so travelers often went out of their way to avoid the allegedly haunted area.

It turns out that there was a pasture in the area of the Quaker Meeting House and, on one occasion, a hungry sheep became caught on a fence while trying to reach some tasty tidbit beyond it. The sheep moaned and groaned while trying to free itself. A traveler happened by who could not determine what the creepy sound was and a rumor spread that the area was haunted. The Quakers helping with the Underground Railroad did nothing to dispel the rumor as a way of keeping superstitious slave catchers at bay.

Another Quaker, Derek Updegraff, was active in the Underground Railroad in the Williamsport area. He offered sanctuary at the Long Reach Plantation, located in the South Reach Road area of Williamsport. Updegraff's uncle Thomas and his great uncle Abraham were also conductors on the Underground Railroad.

The runaway slaves arrived on packet boats at the docks of downtown Williamsport along the Susquehanna River and would be hidden at Updegraff's Exchange Hotel. The president of the Williamsport-Elmira Railroad, Robert Fairies, also was a dedicated abolitionist and used his access to an actual railroad to hide runaway slaves in the baggage compartments of trains going north. In Muncy, the McCarty-Wertman House on Main Street served as another hiding place for slaves seeking freedom.

Lycoming County can be very proud of its extensive and critical role in the Underground Railroad, as the home of many courageous and dedicated citizens who unselfishly toiled for the freedom of others.

Struggle for Civil Rights

As the Civil War concluded, the struggle for equality and civil rights continued. Many events and incidents dealing with this area's African-American heritage virtually have been lost to history.

On November 14 and 15, 1867, African-American activist Frederick Douglass delivered speeches at Doebler's Hall, formerly located at the corner of West Fourth and Pine Streets. Douglass began life as a slave in Maryland and rose in prominence to become an intimate to presidents and later U.S. Minister to Haiti. The noted figure had a leonine appearance with a sweeping gray beard that gave him the look of a biblical prophet. He was a tireless campaigner for the cause of civil rights and the advancement and improvement of African Americans, and was campaigning for these rights when he spoke in Williamsport.

In his first speech, he detailed his "simple plan for elevating the Negro." To whites in the audience he asked, "that blacks be let alone to forge their own position in society, that they be given a fair chance." Douglass implored, "If you see him going to school, let him alone. If you see him going into a mechanic shop to learn a trade, let him alone. If you see him going to the ballot box, let him alone. Give him a chance to let him work out his own position." To blacks he urged, "steady persevering work is the only road to greatness. Nature does the most for them that use the best means."

His second speech the following night chided the federal government for its failure to enact legislation that would give blacks the right to vote, and he advocated women's suffrage more than a half-century before it became the law of the land with the 19th Amendment to the U.S. Constitution. "A man's rights rest in three boxes. The ballot box, jury box, and the cartridge box. Let no man be kept from the ballot box because of his color. Let no woman be kept from the ballot box because of her sex," he said.

Douglass and all African Americans got their wish three years later when the 15th Amendment was ratified, giving blacks the right to vote. To observe this momentous occasion, blacks across Pennsylvania organized celebrations marking the milestone on April 26, 1870. The Williamsport *Gazette and Bulletin* wrote of this celebration in its April 27, 1870 issue:

> Never before yesterday was such a sight as a demonstration of enfranchised colored citizens in the city of Williamsport. Never before yesterday did a body of colored voters assemble together in a deliberative assembly in this city. They will look back upon this day as the most worthy of remembrance among all the events of their strange, but triumphant career.

November 14 and 15, 1867, African-American activist Frederick Douglass delivered speeches at Doebler's Hall, formerly located at the corner of West Fourth and Pine Streets. (JVBL.)

In Williamsport, hundreds of people lined city streets to watch a procession of 41 carriages and buggies, and people carrying banners, some that read, "Equal Rights," "Free Suffrage," and "Virtue, Liberty and Independence."

One carriage carried E.W. Capron, editor and publisher of the *Daily and Weekly Bulletin* and the *West Branch Bulletin*; Abraham Updegraff, president of the First National Bank and former conductor on the underground railroad; J.B.G. Kinsloe, a fellow editor with Capron; and Cornelius Gilchrist, a black laborer. In another wagon, there were little girls sitting around someone dressed as the Goddess of Liberty, waving flags bearing the names of the states that ratified the 15th Amendment. When the parade ended, three and a half hours later, speeches were given by Capron and Updegraff.

Capron said, "We are here to celebrate a day when the Negro, freed and enfranchised can hold up his head and say, I am no longer a slave. I am a man. I can take the ballot in my hand and march to the polls, and there count as much as the president, or any man in the world."

Updegraff followed, "We will no longer address you as colored men but as fellow citizens. You are here today as heirs and joint heirs to the privilege that the 15th Amendment confers on you. Remember my dear friends the price with which this boon has been purchased through the terrible war through which we passed."

A frontier family, living in the outskirts of Williamsport during the 1850s, visits the town for supplies. (JVBL.)

7. Williamsport and the Civil War

In the presidential election of 1860, Abraham Lincoln carried Lycoming County, receiving 3,494 votes to Stephen Douglas's 2,541. Shortly after the election, in an attempt to influence its readers with biased editorials and news columns in the daily newspaper, *The Lycoming Gazette* of February 20, 1861 bitterly attacked Lincoln, reporting that his speeches contained "neither statesmanship, tact, nor talent in them—only twaddle that the merest pettifogger in several counties around would be ashamed to have set down as coming from him, and which the whole nation would blush to know came from the one who is soon to be its chief magistrate."

It was not the first time, nor would it be the last, that a President was so derisively put down for a perceived lack of intelligence, only to have events change that view. The editorials began supporting the President's military policies after Rebel forces fired the first shots of America's bloodiest conflict on the Union garrison at Fort Sumter, South Carolina, in 1861.

With patriotic fervor, Lycoming County answered President Lincoln's call for troops to put down the rebellion by the Confederate States. Within 12 days, Lycoming mustered three companies of 244 men for service to the Union. When the companies departed from the Pine Street Railroad Depot, located near the corner of present-day Pine Street and Little League Boulevard, all places of business in Williamsport closed, and the people of Williamsport gave the soldiers a rapturous send-off. According to *Lycoming Gazette* accounts of the time, the crowd exceeded anything ever before seen in Williamsport: "Both of the Williamsport bands were out. At 8:30 the train moved out amid the cheers and tears of the entire people of the town. Ladies' handkerchiefs and men's hats waved everywhere."

In his *History of Lycoming County*, John Meginness wrote, "When war came the enthusiasm of the people broke forth in flame. Monster meetings were held and the citizens demonstrated in the most unmistakable manner they were solid for the Union."

The pay of soldiers ranged from $22 for corporals, to $21 for musicians, and $20 for privates. Higher paid officers were required to furnish their own uniforms and supplies from their salary, but privates were issued the necessities. The first

Lycoming County soldiers to report for service had to wait several months before receiving their uniforms and gear, however, and they often were dependent upon neighboring communities to provide food.

They had worn their oldest clothes in the expectation that they would be provided uniforms upon arrival. More than a month after their arrival in Harrisburg, one soldier wrote a letter to a county newspaper:

> Thus far no uniforms have been furnished us—no shoes, no caps, or clothing of any kind—except perhaps in a few instances; some of the officers have supplied the wants of the most needy of their men from their own private purses; others cannot appear on parade in consequence of a want of clothing. Our rations have been tolerably good until quite recently, when were served the other morning with hard crackers instead of bread, and salt meat, with half-browned coffee. The crackers were soon flying in every direction and shouts of disapprobation rent the air.

A correspondent for the *Philadelphia Evening Bulletin* was impressed with the Lycoming soldiers and wrote about them to his paper:

Several Lycoming County area Civil War soldiers are pictured at an unknown campsite during the war. (JVBL.)

> The 11th Regiment was reported at Harrisburg to be the best drilled regiment in the camp. It is not uniformed and the men are armed with very diversified and wonderful weapons. Some firelocks that I have observed with them might have done service in the old Colonial wars. A few have no guns at all, but are provided with carving and sheath knives, veteran horse-pistols, rusty bayonets and swords that seem to have been beaten into shape in some village forge. What they lack in martial means they make up in physical excellence, as all are broad chested, huge limbed men with countenances already indurated and scarred by a lifetime battle with the elements. . . . They have ponderous feet, if boots are testimonies, and might answer for grenadiers for Frederick the Great.

The 11th Regiment Volunteers participated in almost all of the engagements of the Army of the Potomac.

ON THE HOMEFRONT

On the homefront, those exempt from military service contributed in other ways. A Citizens Committee was established to assist in caring for the families of the fighting men. The committee passed a resolution to borrow bonds "for the purpose of caring for the families who have taken the field in defense of our government."

Williamsport landlords proclaimed a moratorium on the paying of rents while the renting families had men fighting in the field. The *Lycoming Gazette* reported, "Whenever a man quits an employment to go into his country's service his employer will religiously hold the same place open for him until he comes home again."

Lycoming County's women displayed great patriotism by organizing committees to feed soldiers who would be passing through Williamsport on their way to the great staging areas in Harrisburg and Washington, D.C. The Northern Central Railroad that passed through Williamsport was a major artery for transporting troops from the north and northwest, helping to highlight Lycoming County's strategic location. Women placed portable tables in the downtown area nearest the train depots, and the tables groaned under the weight of cold meat, bread, buttermilk, various fresh vegetables, young onions, as well as lager beer and various distilled spirits.

The women also formed Ladies Aid Societies and almost every church had a ladies' auxiliary that contributed to the Union war effort by knitting socks, rolling bandages, and knitting other clothing for the soldiers. Not many women were used as nurses until later, as the war dragged on. At first, the idea of women ministering to the needs of men was too much for the Victorian sensibilities of the time. It was only after extensive lobbying efforts by women like Clara Barton and Dorothea Dix that women were given wider opportunities to nurse the wounded and sick back to health. Then, as troop trains returned through Lycoming County with many wounded soldiers, women of the area did their tender best to aid their brave soldiers in recovering from the ravages of war.

Sadly, the first Civil War–related casualties in Lycoming County occurred four months before the actual commencement of hostilities. In January 1861, members of the Woodward Guards, an elite company of Lycoming County militia, were celebrating Major Robert Anderson's successful evacuation of Fort Moultrie to Fort Sumter in Charleston Harbor. They celebrated by firing a salute with a 12-pound Napoleon cannon. The celebration turned to tragedy as the cannon prematurely fired, maiming and killing two members of the unit.

There are no exact figures for the number of Lycoming County men who served in the Civil War. The only figures that exist are those gathered after Williamsport was made a manpower depot for the Congressional District on May 12, 1863. According to the statistics produced by this depot, which operated until April 14, 1865, Lycoming County furnished 2,481 men for service to the Union. As it did in the rest of the country, the Civil War helped Williamsport and Lycoming County gain a greater sense of nationhood.

STATE SENATOR HENRY JOHNSON

Henry Johnson, a mostly forgotten state senator from Lycoming County, may have played a pivotal role in helping to gain President Lincoln reelection in the tough campaign of 1864.

Johnson was born in Newton, New Jersey on June 12, 1819. He came from a distinguished background. His great-grandfather was Revolutionary War hero General Daniel Brodhead, who served in the Continental Congress and was later assigned by General George Washington to command Continental troops in western Pennsylvania. Brodhead also fought Native Americans in the aftermath of the Great Runaway of 1778.

Johnson graduated from Princeton in 1841 and later that year moved to Muncy, where his mother owned some property. He opened a law practice that operated successfully for 50 years. Active and prominent in political affairs, first as a member of the Whig Party and later as a Republican, he was an early supporter of the Zachary Taylor-Millard Fillmore Whig ticket in the 1848 election, serving in Pennsylvania's Electoral College.

Johnson served during the Civil War as a member of Company K, 14th Pennsylvania Militia, refusing any higher rank than private. His company saw action at the Battle of Antietam, near Hagerstown, Maryland, in September 1862—the bloodiest one-day campaign in American military history. The experience may have helped to shape another campaign he fought in the halls and chambers of the Pennsylvania Senate.

Elected to the senate in 1860, Johnson's district included Lycoming, Clinton, Union, and Centre Counties. In 1864, he became chairman of the Senate Judiciary Committee, at the time the most powerful position in the Senate,

A U.S. Civil War Rally is held outside the Lycoming County Courthouse during the war, about 1861–1865. (LCHS.)

and was Speaker Pro Tem. That year, the Pennsylvania Supreme Court ruled as unconstitutional an 1812 law providing the vote to military personnel who were deployed away from their home states. Since soldiers of voting age were likely to support Lincoln, the ruling endangered the incumbent president's chances of winning Pennsylvania in his reelection bid later that year. Some historians have speculated that the court's decision may have been for political reasons, since a majority of its justices were Democrats, appointed by Democratic governors. Johnson sought to remedy the problem through passage of "a joint resolution proposing an amendment of the Constitution extending the right of suffrage to citizens in actual military service."

Johnson said, "The bill simply contemplates incorporating into the constitution of the state a great measure of remedial justice to our patriotic and brave soldiers in the field, made necessary by a decision of the Supreme Court."

He shepherded the legislation through to passage and the voters of the Commonwealth approved the measure in time for Pennsylvania's soldiers to vote. The action may have been the difference in Lincoln's victory. He carried Pennsylvania with 296,389 votes or 51.75 percent to General George McClellan's 276,308 votes or 48.20 percent, a razor-thin margin of a little more than 20,000 votes.

In *History of Lycoming County*, Meginness wrote that Johnson's "official acts constitute a record of patriotism, ability and zeal, which will endure as long as the Constitution itself."

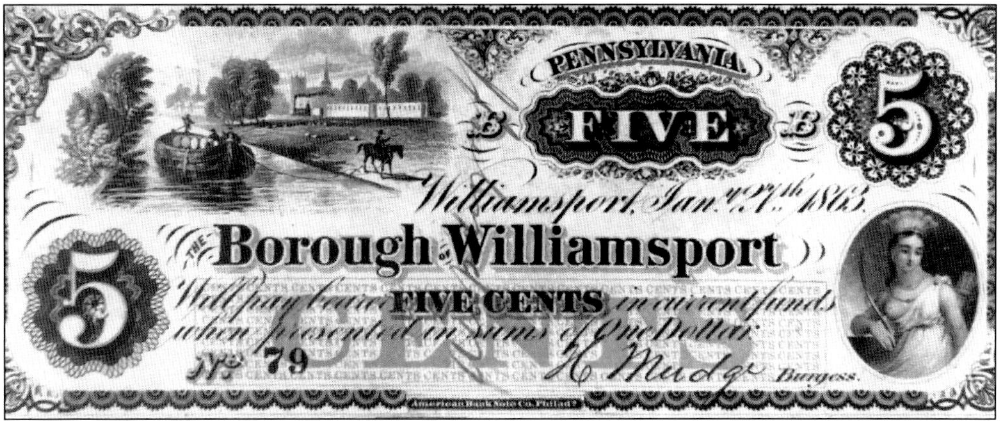

Scrip was issued by Williamsport in 1863 during the Civil War in denominations of 5, 10, 25, and 50¢. The $1 scrip carried the signature of Hiram Mudge, Williamsport's burgess, or mayor. Local scrip was later issued at the height of the Great Depression in 1933. (JVBL.)

LYCOMING MILITARY FIGURES

One of the most distinguished and interesting military figures produced by Lycoming County was Lieutenant Colonel William Butler Beck, son of John and Mary Beck. The Becks moved to Williamsport in 1839, where John Beck opened a tailor shop. He became active in Democratic Party politics and served as Lycoming County sheriff, state legislator, and senator.

William Beck attended Williamsport schools and later Dickinson Seminary (now Lycoming College). He received an appointment to the U.S. Military Academy at West Point in 1855, signed by Secretary of War Jefferson Davis, who would later gain ignominy as the president of the Confederate States of America. Beck resigned from West Point for an unknown reason on October 24, 1856.

He returned to Williamsport and continued his interest in military matters by becoming a charter member and a first lieutenant in the Woodward Guards, one of the first local units to depart at the outbreak of the Civil War. The guards were integrated into the Pennsylvania Militia as Company A, 11th Pennsylvania Volunteers. Like many other members of the Woodward Guards, Beck stayed with his unit longer than called for in his original commitment. He later served with the 5th Artillery in the Regular Army, eventually becoming commander of Battery H. He saw action at such battles as Brandy Station, the Wilderness, Spottsylvania Courthouse, Cold Harbor, and Petersburg.

Beck gained the reputation as an efficient officer and received several brevet promotions for gallantry and meritorious service. He was promoted to captain in October 1864, major in March 1865, and later to lieutenant colonel. Abraham Lincoln and Secretary of War Edwin Stanton signed the promotion papers—priceless wartime documents that were held, for a time, at the Lycoming County Historical Society, but have since disappeared.

Numerous Lycoming County soldiers were held prisoner by the Confederates during the course of the war. Charles A. Rubright, born in Prussia on May 14, 1842, is one of the most notable examples. He and his family emigrated to Jarrettsville, Maryland in 1845. Rubright's father died in 1850 and his mother remarried to Daniel Dorman. In 1856, they moved to Williamsport where Rubright was apprenticed in the spring of 1857 to the bricklaying trade of the Phillip Hoffman firm.

When Lincoln called for troops in the spring of 1861, Rubright was among the first to answer the call. He enlisted as a private and eventually became chief of engineers of the 106th Pennsylvania Volunteer Infantry Regiment, seeing action at the Battle of Gettysburg. Rubright's luck ran out on June 22, 1864 when he was captured during General Ulysses S. Grant's siege of Petersburg, Virginia. He would be held in three of the Confederates' most infamous camps, first at Libby Prison in Richmond, a former cotton warehouse that held 1,200 men in eight crowded, vermin-infested rooms. He also was held at Belle Island, another camp near Richmond. On July 10, 1864, he was transported to the most notorious of all Confederate prison camps, Andersonville, located in Sumter County, Georgia.

Charles A. Rubright, chief of engineers of the 106th Pennsylvania Volunteer Infantry Regiment, saw action at the Battle of Gettysburg but was captured June 22, 1864, in Petersburg, Virginia. He was held at Confederate prison camps Libby Prison and Belle Island, both in Richmond, and at Andersonville, Georgia. (WSG/GRIT.)

Andersonville was a virtual hell on earth. At its height, the camp held almost 40,000 men, of which 13,705 died—most because of the atrocious living conditions. Andersonville's commandant, Henry Wirz, was executed after the war for war crimes, the first such trial in American military history.

Rubright was liberated from Andersonville on April 28, 1865. At the time of his release, he weighed only 85 pounds. He returned from the war with his constitution shattered and his health seriously hampered, but he did not let his horrible war experiences deter him. He became an architect and builder and opened a successful brickworks. According to the *Lycoming Atlas*, Rubright was responsible for designing and building several of Williamsport's most notable public and private buildings, including two railroad depots, all "monuments to his skill and enterprise."

Rubright also was in business for a time as a grocery wholesaler, running Rubright-Hill and Company. He suffered severe financial reverses during the Financial Panic of 1873, but bounced back from this experience with perseverance and skill.

Another infamous Civil War prison camp was located only 70 miles from Williamsport, in Elmira, New York. The Elmira Prison Camp was opened on July 6, 1864 and the last prisoners departed from there on September 27, 1865. According to an article in the *Chemung County Historical Journal* by Thomas Byrne, 12,123 Confederate prisoners were held at Elmira Prison during its existence. Of this number, 2,963 died. Ironically, ex-slave John W. Jones was in charge of the burial of the Confederate dead.

The Civil War Bucktails held its first reunion in October 1887 in Williamsport. The Bucktails were a regiment raised from men in northwestern and Northcentral Pennsylvania who distinguished themselves at various engagements throughout the Civil War. (LCHS.)

The thinning ranks of aged Civil War veterans from the Reno Post of the Grand Army of the Republic gather in front of their post home for the 50th anniversary of the Battle of Gettysburg in 1913. (WSG/GRIT.)

Hundreds of the prisoners held at Elmira passed through Williamsport on their way to internment. On one occasion in 1864, a train carrying prisoners passed by Dickinson Seminary (now Lycoming College) where a number of students from wealthy Southern families were shielded from the dangers of war. Some of the students took out long-hidden Confederate flags and waved them from their rooms at the passing prisoners. The prisoners were heartened by this display, but the demonstration resulted in numerous fights between the Southern students and their pro-Union counterparts.

CIVIL WAR HERO JOHN MUSSER

The Grand Army of the Republic was an organization of Civil War veterans located in towns and cities throughout the Northern States of the Union. It was the Civil War equivalent of the American Legion or Veterans of Foreign Wars. The posts were named for various local Civil War heroes, and the Muncy post, named for John Dunn Musser, was no exception.

Musser was born in Lewisburg on April 24, 1826, and married his cousin Ellie E. Bowman on October 24, 1855. Unfortunately, she died several days after giving

A group of African-America Civil War veterans from the Grand Army of the Republic Fribley Post head out to march in a Memorial Day parade in 1912. (WSG/GRIT.)

birth on June 10, 1857 to their only child, Ellie Bowman Musser. Some reports indicate that during one period before his marriage, from 1849 to 1851, Musser sought his fortune in California's gold fields.

When the Civil War broke out in the spring of 1861, Musser did not immediately enlist. He was torn by a sense of duty to his motherless young daughter and to commonwealth and country. By the summer of 1862, Musser enlisted, entrusting his young daughter to her grandparents, Mr. and Mrs. Joshua Bowman.

Musser was commissioned a first lieutenant of Company K, 143rd Regiment, Pennsylvania Infantry, and a month later he was promoted to major. According to Robert T. Lyon in his article on Musser in *Now and Then*, the journal of the Muncy Historical Society, "The 143rd Regiment, Pa. Volunteers was one of the most active of the nearly 250 regiments from Pennsylvania that served during the war." Mexican War veteran Colonel Edmund L. Dana commanded the regiment.

The Musser/Bowman family sent several of its members to Union service during the war. Musser's brother-in-law Washington Dunn Bowman was killed at the Battle of Fredericksburg in January 1863. Musser's brother Robert, a captain, was captured near Manassas Station, Virginia, while trying to keep supplies from falling in Confederate hands. Captain Musser was exchanged later that year. Another Musser brother, William, served as an army surgeon and was stationed near Washington, D.C.

Musser became executive officer of the 143rd Regiment and saw action at the battles of Fredericksburg and Chancellorsville, but it would be at the Battle of Gettysburg that he would distinguish himself. The 143rd was attached to General John Reynolds's First Corps. When Reynolds was killed on the first day of the battle, General Abner Doubleday took command of the I Corps; Dana, commander of the 143rd Regiment, assumed command of the brigade. Command of the 143rd Regiment fell to Musser.

The 143rd played a critical role in repulsing the Confederates at Seminary Ridge on the first day of the battle, July 1, 1863. The charges and countercharges kept him in the thick of the fray. Entering the battle, the 143rd had 465 men; they lost 262.

Musser emerged from the bloody fight unscathed, though he had two horses shot out from under him. According to Lyon's article in *Now and Then,* Musser filed a claim with the Lycoming Mutual Insurance Company for the cost of the horses. Musser's father-in-law Joshua Bowman was a member of the board of directors of the same insurance company at the time the claim was filed. The United States government paid the estate of John Musser $200 for the cost of the horses killed.

Musser, then a lieutenant colonel, returned home on furlough in January 1864 to see his young daughter, but he would never see her again. Back at the front in April, a "certificate of disability" was sent to his commanding officer, detailing a condition that resembled severe, chronic bronchitis and stated, "therefore he is unfit for duty." Apparently, either Musser or his superiors disregarded the certificate because he returned to action with his regiment in Virginia at the Battle of the Wilderness the first week of May 1864. On May 3, Musser's commanding officer was wounded

A flooded Pine Street is pictured during the flood of March 17, 1865, the first of the great floods to be recorded with a still camera. (LCHS.)

and taken prisoner, and Musser assumed command. On the morning of May 6, Musser was mortally wounded when his femoral artery was struck by a minié ball. He died at the division hospital, and his body was returned to Muncy where it was interred in the Muncy Cemetery, next to his wife and brother-in-law.

In God We Trust

Another bit of Civil War–era lore concerns James Pollock, who quite literally left his mark on U.S. currency.

Pollock entered public service as Northumberland County District Attorney in 1835 and served until 1838. He was elected as a Whig to the U.S. Congress in 1844, and during his tenure was a strong advocate for a trans-continental railroad. He was part of a group that encouraged Samuel F.B. Morse and his new invention, the telegraph.

One of Pollock's good friends while serving in Congress was fellow Whig Abraham Lincoln, an association that would serve Pollock well in later years. After leaving Congress in 1849, Pollock returned to private legal practice but did not retire from the public realm. On January 15, 1851, he was appointed president judge of the Eighth Judicial District, including Northumberland, Lycoming, Columbia, and Sullivan Counties, to fill the unexpired term of the late Judge Joseph Biles Anthony. He was nominated by a coalition of Whigs, Abolitionists, and Know Nothings to run for governor of Pennsylvania in 1854, winning by more than 40,000 votes.

Pollock's term was regarded as a "clean and progressive one." In his inaugural address, he set out his view of America during a time of sectional strife when he said, "Freedom is the great law of American nationality. Slavery is the exception, local and sectional."

He was an advocate of public education and signed legislation establishing the State Normal School system. Normal Schools were the predecessors of the state college and later the state university system. In 1855, he signed the permanent charter of the Farmer's High School, later to become Pennsylvania State University, and was instrumental in choosing its location at State College. Pollock also established the Department of Public Instruction, which later became the Department of Education, one of the earliest and most successful education systems established in the United States.

Pollock chose not to run for reelection as governor, and the legislature escorted him, en masse, to the Harrisburg train station for his journey north to Milton. Williamsport resident William F. Packer succeeded him as governor.

Pollock remained in private life for only a short time. In January 1861, President James Buchannan appointed him a member of the Crittenden Commission, whose purpose was to avert war through compromise. Unfortunately, their work was in vain.

When Pollock's old congressional friend Lincoln became President in March 1861, Pollock was appointed director of the U.S. Mint in Philadelphia. In 1864, Pollock proposed that all U.S. coins bear the inscription, "In God We Trust." The proposal met with favor from Secretary of the Treasury Salmon P. Chase and Lincoln.

Pollock resigned in 1866, but in 1869 President Ulysses S. Grant reappointed him as the mint's director, where he served until 1873. President Rutherford B. Hayes appointed Pollock as the chief naval officer of the Philadelphia Naval District in 1879 where he served until 1883. Pollock died on April 19, 1890 in Lock Haven at the age of 80. The epitaph on his tombstone appropriately reads, "James Pollock 1810–1890, In God We Trust."

THE REPASZ BAND

Daniel Repasz was born in Clinton Township, Lycoming County, on April 18, 1813. He later lived in Muncy, became a tailor by trade, and took up the violin. He moved to Williamsport in 1838, teaching music and dancing. He took lessons from A.K. Mabie, the director of the Williamsport Band, the musical entity that would later be renamed for Repasz. Founded in 1831 by Jacob C. Mussina, the band consisted initially of flutes, clarinets, piccolos, and a French horn. Repasz joined the band in 1840, playing the "keyed bugle," a cross between a trumpet and a clarinet. He became the band's director in 1856, introducing new instruments and innovative musical arrangements. Under his baton, the band gained prominence and toured the Northeast extensively, and it took his name as its own.

When the Civil War began in April 1861, the Repasz Band enlisted as a body, not uncommon in those days. Members spent most of the war attached to the

Daniel Repasz was the founder and namesake of American's oldest community band, the Repasz Band. (LCHS.)

8th Pennsylvania Cavalry. The band "dueled" with a Confederate band at General Robert E. Lee's surrender at Appomattox. The Confederate band played "Dixie," and "Bonnie Blue Flag," countered by the Repasz Band's "Battle Cry of Freedom" and the "Star Spangled Banner."

Repasz died on April 18, 1891, but his lasting legacy lives on in the Repasz Band, which still performs locally and regionally. The band played at the dedication of Grant's Tomb in New York City on April 27, 1897, and returned to play there at a ceremony 100 years later.

This piece of sheet music for the "Repasz Band March" was produced by the Vandersloot Music Company in Williamsport. Vandersloot was one of the leading producers of sheet music in the country at one time during the early 1900s. (LCHS.)

8. Industrial Development

Industrial developments that began in Lycoming County during the Civil War accelerated after 1865, along with the rest of the country. In 1860, 430 manufacturing establishments could boast a capital investment of more than $2 million in the region, but ten years later, there were 608 factories and capital investment had tripled. Within a few years, the transcontinental railroad linked two coasts of the continent, as millions of immigrants from Europe and China filled the ranks of America's postwar industrial working class.

One keen businessman who profited during the Civil War as a sutler (a person who traveled with armies and provided its stores) was Layton Legg Stearns. In 1850, Stearns and his brother-in-law L.N. Muir moved to northcentral Pennsylvania and opened a retail establishment in Jersey Shore, selling everything from clothespins to drugs and chemicals. When the Civil War began, he followed the soldiers of the 8th Pennsylvania Cavalry, selling provisions such as tobacco, soap, stationery, and food.

In the fall of 1865, Stearns began a retail venture in Williamsport, bringing his family and all of his merchandise down the river by raft from Jersey Shore. He bought a dry goods and grocery business at the corner of West Third and Market Streets, but by 1885, his flourishing store had outgrown itself. He bought the old City Hotel at the corner of Third and Pine Streets in 1888, and admitted his three sons into partnership. On October 11, 1889, L.L. Stearns and Sons opened as one of the most progressive and modern stores in the region, and continued operating for nearly 100 years. The store boasted electric lights and elevators, and a vacuum tube whisked sales slips and payments to the cashier's office. Stearns, always willing to experiment and try new methods, was among the first stores to place price tags on goods. When Williamsport's merchant prince died on January 3, 1906, all dry goods stores in downtown Williamsport closed between 2 p.m. and 3 p.m. as a mark of respect.

First Grange in Pennsylvania

In Lycoming County, the state's leading agricultural organization established its first chapter in 1871: the Order of the Patrons of Husbandry, better known as the

Layton Legg Stearns, Williamsport's "Merchant Prince" and founder of Williamsport's most famous department store, began as a sutler during the Civil War. (JVBL.)

Grange. Oliver H. Kelley and a group of six other concerned farmers founded the National Grange organization on November 15, 1867 to serve the interests of farmers and agriculture-related issues and to promote fellowship. Patterned after a secret society like the Masonic Order, it would have seven degrees, four of them representing the four seasons of the year, and would utilize rituals much like the Masons.

Unlike the Masons, however, the Grange founders thought that it was important to have women as well as young people involved. They determined the best way to promote the new organization was to send a "lecturer" or "deputy" into farming areas and to tell the story of the Grange, which literally means a house with a farm attached.

The Grange movement also was formed as a reaction to the economic realities of the late 1860s and 1870s. Monopoly capitalists like J.P. Morgan controlled banking and railroad interests, squeezing small farmers with high interest rates, rail shipping costs, and storage fees for crops. Grangers united to put political pressure on state legislatures and the U.S. Congress to regulate the large economic interests.

Luke Eger was a Montgomery-area farmer who discovered the Grange movement through farm magazines, including *The Prairie Farmer.* He wrote to Grange founder Oliver Kelley for information, promoting the movement among his neighbors and friends, and in March 1871, Colonel D.D. Curtiss, representing the National Grange, presided over the chartering of Pennsylvania's first Grange: Eagle Grange No. 1. That Grange exists today, as do seven others in Lycoming County.

WILLIAM ELLIOT AND HIS ACADEMY OF MUSIC

In 1870, William G. Elliot, a city native born on July 19, 1840, returned as a successful businessman after making a fortune in the oil business. He built a three-story building at the corner of West Fourth and Pine Streets that became the Academy of Music, containing a number of stores, offices, and lodge rooms.

Eliot was the express manager for the Philadelphia & Reading Railroad from 1872 until 1879. In 1892, he was elected mayor of Williamsport, and during his four-year term he helped the city recover from the disastrous flood of 1894. He also helped set in motion the drive to build a new city hall on Pine Street. Eliot was aggressive in having many of the city's streets paved, sewers installed, and other infrastructure improvements. He died on December 20, 1905.

HIRAM RHOADS: UTILITY INNOVATOR

Unabated growth was checked in 1873 when the country suffered a severe industrial depression. The gulf widened between great wealth and opulence, and poverty and tribulation, helping to revive the labor movement. Still, the 1870s were a time of great innovation and the introduction of many inventions in America. Williamsport started early in the use of one of those new inventions—the telephone—when, in 1879, it set up its first exchange. The man who made that possible was Hiram R. Rhoads.

Rhoads was born on March 29, 1845, in Philadelphia. His family moved to Lycoming County in 1859 and he served in the Civil War with the 4th Pennsylvania Volunteer Militia Regiment. Later, Rhoads excelled in his work as a telegraph operator for the Pennsylvania Railroad, and by the time he left the railroad in 1878, he was chief telegrapher of the Eastern Division.

He became an agent for the fledgling Bell Telephone Company and was responsible for developing the second telephone exchange in the state, the first being in Erie. The Williamsport exchange started operations on May 1, 1879, well received because of the many wealthy residents who wanted the latest technological toys as part of a never-ending search for status. Rhoads worked tirelessly to convince financial giants, and others more humble, of the benefits of having a telephone. His unswerving faith in the telephone helped to make Williamsport an early success with the innovation.

The new telephone exchange consisted of 385 miles of wire, with 107 residences and 445 businesses involved for a total of 582 telephones in the city. Later, the exchange added 23 phones in Jersey Shore and 20 in Muncy. That phone exchange was owned for its first year by Rhoads, but on October 1, 1880,

One of the first orders of business for county commissioners after establishing Lycoming County was the building of the Lycoming County Courthouse. This photo, taken in the 1890s, shows telephone and telegraph poles with wires sprouting from them. (JVBL.)

Rhoads and several other investors opened the Central Pennsylvania Telephone and Supply Company. It incorporated with an authorized capital of $1 million, with Rhoads as its president, Richard O'Brien as vice president, and R.M. Bailey as general manager.

Rhoads was also founder of the Lycoming Electric Company, president of the Williamsport Passenger Railway Company, and instrumental in the conversion of the company's streetcars from horse-driven to electric powered. He was a director and organizer of the Merchants' National Bank, a founder of the Ross Club, and prominent in Masonic circles.

Like many distinguished men of his time, he had a home designed by noted architect Eber Culver. He married Mary E. Howell in 1868 and they had four daughters. Rhoads seemed to have a continued bright future ahead of him when he died on February 17, 1894 of a heart ailment at the age of 49.

BRANDON PARK: GIFT OF ANDREW BOYD CUMMINGS

For generations, Williamsporters have enjoyed the lush greenery and open spaces of Brandon Park, but few know of the man who is responsible for it, the virtually forgotten Andrew Boyd Cummings. Born in Williamsport in 1807, his was a prominent Williamsport family that ran one of the city's earliest hotels and established the first mail route in the area. His brother Alexander Cummings attained distinction as a journalist, politician, and legislator, and later served as governor of the Colorado Territory. Cummings also had a sister, Jane, who married John Brandon. In 1829, Cummings partnered with Brandon and assisted in publishing the *Lycoming Chronicle*, one of the early predecessors of the *Sun-Gazette* newspaper.

When Cummings's sister died in 1840 at the age of 34, he was devastated and never entirely recovered. He moved to Philadelphia, where he became a successful businessman, and visits back to Williamsport were few. But he never forgot the place of his birth, where he still had extensive real estate holdings, and in February 1889, Cummings donated more than 43 acres of his land to the city for a park named in honor of his sister. In 1926, the city placed a bas-relief-sculptured image of Cummings and his sister at the entrance of Brandon Park.

EARLY FIREFIGHTING DAYS AND SPECTACULAR FIRES

There have been many disasters and spectacular fires in the history of Williamsport, but one of the most memorable and destructive took place on the eastern fringe of downtown on August 20, 1871. The fire consumed 45 buildings and caused an estimated $300,000 in damage.

Williamsport postman George "Pony Andrews" W. Andrews delivered the mail to outlying districts in 1890 on horseback. (WSG/GRIT.)

Williamsport, in those early days, had four fire companies: Rescue No. 1, Independent No. 1, Neptune No. 2, and Washington No. 2, all organized in 1856. But the primitive quality of firefighting equipment and techniques in those days barely slowed fire's destructive power.

The Rescue and Neptune companies were hand-drawn engines, basically powerful hand pumps. The members lined up along the handles and "jumped" them, augmented by bucket brigades. Each family was required to have a certain number of leather buckets they brought to the scene when the fire alarm was sounded. Forming a line to the nearest source of water, the men passed full buckets toward the fire and women passed the empties back for refilling.

The Great Fire of 1871 began around 8 p.m. when a stable owned by C.M. Baker caught fire on Black Horse Alley (now Church Street). It spread across both sides of Willow Street, between State and East Streets, and raged down Mulberry as far as East Third Street. Embers caught part of the Dickinson Seminary (now Lycoming College) afire. The conflagration raged for hours, could be seen from as far away as Muncy, and smoldered for days.

Some of the notable buildings destroyed or damaged included the old Doebler Hall, a three-story brick building that served as one of Williamsport's first theaters, and the Waverly Hotel. Two of the city's greatest architectural losses were the mansion of the late Governor William Packer and the Russell Inn. The mansion contained an irreplaceable library reputed to be the largest collection of books north of Harrisburg. Russell Inn, in which some of the first court sessions in Lycoming County were held, was the first building erected in Williamsport.

The first firefighters in the city were volunteers and several companies were formed. Early companies dressed colorfully; all wore red uniforms—except for the Hibernia Company, which insisted on wearing green uniforms since most of its members were of Irish descent. The most colorful company was the Darktown Fire Brigade, often described as a minstrel show in fire gear. The company had its own band and dressed in colorful costumes, some of them in black face, white linen dusters, and white stove pipe or plug hats. In 1835, Williamsport received its first fire engine, dubbed "Sassy Sally," a hand pumper with single brakes at each end for pumping water.

Unfortunately, these companies developed serious rivalries and jealousies that hampered firefighting. In 1874, Mayor Martin Powell presented two petitions from prominent citizens urging the council to form a paid fire department, and the council passed the resolution. The ordinance called for a chief engineer and one assistant, with three engine companies and one hose company. The engineer, firemen, and teamster of each company were full-time employees and the foreman and six horsemen were paid as needed. The chief engineer was paid an annual salary of \$500; engineers \$720; firemen \$480; teamsters \$600; foremen \$300; and hosemen \$200. M.H. Caldwell was elected the city's first fire chief and H.M. Page was elected assistant chief.

Original companies in the paid department were Independent No. 1, Washington No.2, Hibernia No. 3, Liberty No. 4, and Keystone Hook and

Ladder No. 1. The first motorized fire engine was purchased in 1911, and in 1914, the first motorized, triple-combination pumper, chemical, and hose wagon was acquired. Two more motorized units came into service in 1918. The fire chief got his first automobile in 1912. Prior to that he responded in a horse and buggy.

The number of city firefighters has declined from a high of 72 in the late 1960s to the current strength of 30 firefighters and 3 fire administrators. At one time, there were seven firehouses in operation, but only one manned fire station now exists in the city.

DIETRICK LAMADE: A SELF-MADE MAN WITH GRIT

For more than 100 years, the *Grit* was a Sunday morning staple as America's favorite family newspaper. Many in small-town America remember the *Grit* with warmth, made possible by a Dietrick Lamade, a German immigrant and self-made man.

Lamade was born on February 6, 1859 in Goelshausen, Germany, one of nine children of Johannes Dietrick and Caroline Stuepfle Lamade. His family immigrated to Williamsport in 1867 at the behest of friends who found

Dietrick Lamade, a self-made man, began and operated the nationally famous Grit *newspaper in Williamsport. (WSG/GRIT.)*

opportunity here. The death of Lamade's father cut short formal education for Dietrick, and at the age of ten he was forced to help support his family. He worked as an errand boy for various stores until, at 13, he began working in the office of a local German-language weekly, *Beobachter*.

At 18, Lamade got his first experience as a publisher. During the holiday season of 1877, he devoted his spare time to producing several issues of *The Merchants' Free Press*, a four-page, free advertising pamphlet. Later he published a theater program, and in the summer of 1880, he published a small paper called the *Camp News*, while the Pennsylvania National Guard bivouacked in Williamsport.

In 1882, Lamade was made an assistant foreman at the plant of the *Daily Sun and Banner* of Williamsport. That year, the paper started a Saturday afternoon publication called *The Grit*. By 1884, he had left the *Sun and Banner* and headed a new weekly publication called *The Times* that was scheduled to become a daily, but ill health and lack of finances by its owner caused it to fold.

Needing work, Lamade gambled and began his own newspaper, with two partners and a combined investment of $1,000. He bought the *Grit* name from the *Sun and Banner* to use for his new publication. The first year of the *Grit* was one of adversity and uncertainty, as it owed more than it was worth, but Lamade did not lose faith. The circulation was about 4,000 and many more subscribers would be needed if the paper were to survive.

Lamade came up with an innovative idea that would save his fledgling newspaper and transform it into a national institution. Coupons in the paper provided chances for readers to win various prizes, including a piano, gold watch, marble-top bedroom suit, rifle, and silk dress. His partners thought his new idea was impractical and costly, but that did not deter him, saying, "difficulties show what men are." From May until November 1885, Lamade traveled all over northcentral Pennsylvania five days a week, using his gift lottery as a foundation for building the statewide circulation of the *Grit*.

He carried two large suitcases of *Grit* advertising materials and convinced many small stores and newsagents to carry the publication. After his week on the road, he returned to the paper's offices and slept on a folding cot on Friday and Saturday nights to ensure that it was shipped to the out-of-town agents on Saturday mornings, and that the Williamsport edition was ready for Sunday mornings.

On Thanksgiving Day 1885, the grand prize drawing was held at Williamsport's Academy of Music with a capacity crowd on hand. Five prizes were given out, three to out-of-towners and two to local residents. Lamade's tireless efforts more than doubled circulation, helping to stabilize the *Grit*'s finances. He expanded circulation even more by using direct mail and hiring newsboys in locations throughout the country to sell the paper.

The *Grit* was one of the first newspapers in America to feature color and fictional supplements. By 1900, it had a national audience, and by the late 1970s, its circulation was more than 1.2 million. Lamade died on October 9, 1938 at the age of 79, a beloved figure mourned by many, and his descendants remain prominent today in Williamsport.

The James V. Brown Library, a gift to a beloved wife, was completed in 1906. It is one of the most dynamic libraries in the Commonwealth. (JVBL.)

JAMES V. BROWN'S LEGACY

The historic *Grit* is preserved on microfilm at Williamsport's James V. Brown Library, where every year thousands of area residents check out books, films, and periodicals. Thousands more use the library's bookmobile and make use of the library's research and computer facilities. But very few give much thought to the man who made it possible, James Vanduzee Brown.

Brown did not attend college, but possessed a great deal of common sense and native ability. He was a strong believer in self-improvement and self-study. He came to Williamsport in 1859 to purchase the Updegraff and Herdic Flour Mill, which he operated until 1866.

Williamsport was in the midst of its lumber boom, and Brown sensed opportunity, selling his interests in the flourmill to became a partner in the lumber firm of James Thompson and Company. He later formed Brown, Early and Company, and erected lumber mills on Park Street. In April 1864, Brown became involved in the activity that, next to the library itself, would have the most lasting impact on the Williamsport area—the Williamsport Water Company.

For its first 11 years, the struggling company was viewed as a poor investment, paying no dividends to investors. It was into that uncertain financial situation that Brown plunged, turning the company into a profitable venture. By 1868, Brown became its president, a position he held for 37 years, risking his fortune to help create a pure-water system that serves people today.

Brown and his wife Carile dreamed of a free public library for the people of Williamsport. Carile Brown and the members of her newly formed chapter of the Daughters of the American Revolution felt strongly that a library was needed for the city, and she may have influenced her husband to use some of his wealth to accomplish that mission. Unfortunately, she did not live to see her dream come true, as she died on November 18, 1902.

Brown spent the next two years designing the library that would bear his name. He envisioned a magnificent marble edifice in the French Renaissance style that was impressive yet simple in design, at the corner of East Fourth and State Streets. Brown, like his wife, did not live to see his dream built. He died on December 8, 1904, at the age of 78. The library opened on June 17, 1907, amid pageantry and fanfare, and has become the crown jewel of the region's library system.

MARY SLAUGHTER: BENEFACTOR OF ELDERLY AFRICAN-AMERICAN WOMEN

Mary Slaughter was born into slavery on the Myers plantation near Martinsburg, Virginia, on February 27, 1835. She remembered these slave days in an interview 88 years later, saying she felt honored to be regarded as the Myers' favorite housekeeper. She said her duties involved cooking, adding that Christmas was always a special time on the plantation because of the extra-special quality of food served during the holiday, with turkey, opossum, apple pie, and finger cakes. But even more special was that slave families on the Myers plantation were permitted to spend the holidays together. Normally, family members would be scattered throughout various sections of the plantation and perhaps even on neighboring plantations, seldom seeing each other. She was a proficient knitter and took a special pride in her work, often knitting her own stockings because she could not afford to buy them.

Religion played an important role in her life, having been baptized within a month of birth, once the ice in the river near the plantation broke. "While slavery was wrong, if the white man had not brought the black to this land how would they have learned about Christ and become Christianized?" she posed.

She married William Slaughter, probably while still on the Myers plantation, and they moved to Williamsport in 1866. They were custodians at St. Paul's Lutheran Church, and she became a member of the First Baptist Church but also was active at the Bethel African Methodist Episcopal Church. She enjoyed the opportunity, as a "free person," to travel where she wanted, taking the opportunity to travel to the nation's centennial celebration in 1876 in Philadelphia. Later she traveled as a delegate to the state Baptist convention in 1889.

She had three children, but they all died early in life. She suffered another loss when her beloved husband died of consumption (tuberculosis) in April 1886. She turned to constructive ways to deal with her grief and continued to show her love for children by furnishing meals for those whose mothers were ill. She opened her four-room, frame house on Walnut Street to the elderly in the late 1890s.

By 1897, her concept evolved into the Aged Colored Women's Home, a place for indigent, elderly African-American women to live out their last years in a dignified, caring setting. In 1899, Mary moved the facility to 124 Brandon Place, where it operated until 1973. One person wrote the following of Slaughter and her home:

> Mrs. Slaughter is doing the work with the aid of other women of the home. She cares for them all, looks after the furnace, cooks all the meals, sees that they are dressed to receive their friends who regularly go to read with them or hold meetings, and she thanks God daily for His goodness to her and her old women.

She originally funded her home through appeals to the community, thanks to her energy, devotion, and sincerity. She then mortgaged her home to finance some renovations for its expansion, but as the needs of her charity increased it became clear to Slaughter that some state aid would be needed for her to continue her good work. With that in mind, the humble former slave went to Harrisburg to lobby legislators for state support, apparently making a positive impression because the state soon allocated funds for the home and its mortgage. State Senator Charles Sones was her greatest champion and worked hard behind the scenes to ensure the appropriation.

In a 1923 interview, she remarked, "If fifty years ago someone told me that I would be living as I am today I would not have thought it possible . . . yes, God is good to me." Slaughter died at the age of 99 in 1934, leaving behind a wonderful legacy of care and compassion for the aged. Despite her death, her home continued to serve elderly women. In 1960, recognizing her contributions, the state officially changed the name to the Mary Slaughter Home.

By 1973, the home was unable to meet the new state code requirements needed to operate homes for the elderly and the facility closed after 75 years of service. The original building was razed and apartments for senior citizens were erected in its place, but Mary wasn't forgotten—the new housing was named the Mary Slaughter Apartments.

AUGUST RICHTER CLEANS THE CITY

Cities were foul and fetid places in the mid- to late 1800s, with open sewers, farm animals wandering about, and other unsanitary intrusions polluting the streets and water supplies. Dr. August Richter sought to change that in Williamsport.

Richter traveled extensively in Europe, an opportunity that provided him with a cosmopolitan view of the world and exposed him to the newest ideas in medicine, hygiene, and sanitation—knowledge that he would later use with great fervor. He came to America in the late 1840s and studied to be a physician at the

Pennsylvania Medical College, graduating in 1851. That same year, he arrived in Williamsport and established a medical practice. In 1871, he became a member of the city board of health, where he began his crusade.

He was a tireless advocate for the establishment of the city's first hospital. When the hospital was built in 1873, he became one of the first members of its board of trustees and was active in its expansion and improvement. In 1887, he was appointed city health officer, a job Richter performed with professionalism, determination and impartiality, sometimes stepping on the toes of the wealthy and influential. "To his untiring zeal and devotion to duty of that office, the city is largely indebted for its freedom from epidemics following the great flood of June 1889," historian Meginness writes.

Richter was temporarily removed from office in December 1889 because of alleged "neglect of duty." There was a complaint regarding an excessive amount of manure in a lot at Vine, Third, and Grier Streets, but when Richter checked the area, all he found was sawdust. A few days later, before he had a chance to check it again, the city health board met to dismiss him. He answered their charges, writing, "Where ignorance prevails . . . the post of honor is a private station."

The controversy died and he was reappointed health officer, serving until 1900, when he was named Lycoming County medical inspector by the state board of

Dr. Jean Saylor Brown was one of the earliest female physicians in Williamsport and worked with Dr. Rita Church and others to found the Williamsport Hospital. (JVBL.)

health. He served for ten years and was one of the first doctors in the state to inspect dairy farms for sanitary conditions.

Richter married Cecilia Steuber in 1883, and they had five children, one of whom died in infancy. Richter died at the age of 88 on February 20, 1910.

PIONEERS OF THE MEDICAL PROFESSION

Two of the first female doctors in Williamsport, Rita Biansia Church and Jean Saylor Brown, were pioneers in the area's medical profession, both involved in notable firsts in Lycoming County's medical history and both inextricably linked.

Church was born in Brookfield, New York, on June 13, 1841. She received her medical degree in 1874 from the Women's Medical College Hospital of Philadelphia, the only medical school in the country training women physicians at the time. While there, Church made a friendship with the person that would have the strongest impact on her career: Jean Saylor, later Jean Saylor Brown.

Brown was born in Holland, New Jersey, on December 1, 1843. She moved with her parents to Williamsport in 1854 and later entered Dickinson Seminary, today Lycoming College, where she received her bachelor's degree. She, too, graduated from the Women's Medical College in 1874. She returned to

Dr. Rita Church was the first female physician in Williamsport and one of the founders of the Williamsport Hospital, along with Dr. Jean Saylor Brown. (JVBL.)

Williamsport following graduation from medical school and started an extensive, prosperous practice that spread beyond the confines of Lycoming County, and she persuaded Church to bring her medical skills to the Williamsport area as well.

Church and Brown were strong advocates for the welfare of the Williamsport Hospital in its formative years. Church was named the hospital's first superintendent and resident physician on November 9, 1881, for $250 per year. During the next three years, Church and Brown were dynamos who did almost everything to keep the hospital running as efficiently as possible. They prepared their own ointments and suppositories, treating patients with great care and diligence, even though nurses normally would performed such tasks, exposing a critical need for nursing care. Brown and Church became the driving force in the establishment of a school of nursing at the hospital in 1883—only the third nursing education program to be established in the country.

Brown has the historic distinction of performing the first operation "worthy of mention" by a physician in Lycoming County in 1881, and she contributed the first $100 toward the building of an operating room at the hospital. She served on the hospital's board of managers from 1887 to 1896 and was the only woman to serve on that board until 1976. She was prominent in other spheres as well and active in charitable and community service causes. Further, she was one of the founders of the local YWCA.

Church was an able hospital administrator, helping it to recover from its first major crisis—the June 1889 flood. At the time, the hospital was located at Elmira and Walnut Streets, a flood-prone area, which later prompted hospital managers to seek a site on higher ground. During Church's tenure, the hospital began its move to its present location.

Church resigned as hospital superintendent on April 10, 1893, to help with the founding of the Lock Haven Hospital, for which she worked until 1900. She became blind and was confined to a wheelchair, spending the remainder of her days at a nursing home in Elmira, New York.

HIGHER EDUCATION IN WILLIAMSPORT

The son of a farmer, Samuel Transeau was a leader in establishing Williamsport's high school. Born on October 1, 1836 in Northampton County, Transeau was encouraged by his parents, William and Elizabeth Schnabel, to take an interest in education. One of the reasons the family moved from Easton to the eastern part of Lycoming County was so their son might have the opportunity to continue his studies at a more advanced school.

He was trained for the ministry as a Reformed Church pastor by attending the Academy at McEwensville and Franklin and Marshall College. He graduated in 1859, furthering his studies at the theological seminary of the Reformed Church at Mercersburg. In 1862, he became an assistant pastor to the Reverend William Goodrich. He married Laura Zimmerman in 1867 and they had three children.

Transeau moved his family to Williamsport in 1869 and taught at the Franklin School. Soon he was entrusted with organizing a high school, which he began with an enrollment of 13 students. By the end of its second year, it had 75 students. He became the superintendent of city schools in 1875 and oversaw the reorganization of the city school system, as well as the construction of several schools. Transeau died on April 30, 1907.

A LONG, MUDDY WALK

It was a muddy, two-day walk from Milton to Williamsport in the spring of 1847 by the Reverend Benjamin H. Crever that eventually resulted in Lycoming College.

Crever, born March 16, 1817 in Carlisle, was the son of a newspaper editor. He was raised with a strong Lutheran faith and attended Dickinson College in Carlisle. There, he converted to Methodism, a life-altering event. As a member of Carlisle Methodist Episcopal Church, he came under the influence of the Reverend George Cookman, who prompted Crever to be called to the ministry. The Baltimore Conference of the Methodist Church appointed him to a six-week period as a preacher in Staunton, Virginia, and after a stint as a temperance speaker in Virginia, he moved to Baltimore to become one of five ministers to the City Station Church.

Dr. Benjamin Crever was the founder of Dickinson Seminary, later to become Lycoming College. (WSG/GRIT.)

He married Susan Caroline Follansbee, a teacher from New Hampshire, in 1843, and the couple moved to Lewisburg. There, his health declined and he took a temporary break from the ministry. Crever did not wish to remain idle, however, and he and his family moved to Milton to operate a school.

He had a dream of establishing a denominational school that would be supervised by the Baltimore Conference of the Methodist Church. He heard that the Williamsport Academy, established in 1812, was for sale, so he walked to Williamsport to make an offer. He purchased it on behalf of the Methodist church, whose officials originally offered Crever a job as principal. He turned them down and suggested Dr. Thomas Bowman, and Crever became the school's financial agent and a teacher of experimental sciences. His wife became the preceptress, or dean, of the school. The school was called Dickinson Seminary because of the preparatory relationship it had with Dickinson College in Carlisle. It had 212 students in its first year.

Susan Crever died in 1886 and Benjamin Crever died on April 15, 1890, after an extended illness. He and his wife are interred in the Williamsport Cemetery on Washington Boulevard, not far from the school that he helped to found.

The former Williamsport High School, located at the corner of West Third and Walnut Streets, is lost to the flames in an April 1914 fire. That building was due to be vacated at the end of the school year and a new building at West Third and Susquehanna Streets opened in the fall of 1914. (JVBL.)

WILLIAMSPORT'S PROHIBITIONIST MAYOR

James Mansel's prohibitionist tendencies would propel him into a political prominence he never really sought. The late nineteenth century saw a variety of civic and personal improvement movements; the most important was the prohibitionist or temperance movement. The advocates of prohibition sought the banning of intoxicating liquor because they deemed it a blight on society, producing indolence, family violence, economic inefficiency, and the squandering of hard-earned money, and its adherents slowly acquired political power. On February 18, 1896, a hotly contested and divisive Williamsport mayoral election featured five candidates, including Mansel.

Mansel won the race with 2,257 votes to 1,909 for Republican Samuel N. Williams (who would succeed him as mayor). Democrat Alvin S. Corle received 1,420 votes and Independent candidate W.L. Parker had 33. Mansel became the city's 13th chief executive and was the first Prohibitionist elected as mayor in the state, serving as mayor from 1896 to 1899. His administration received the reputation, according to a *Grit* editorial of February 4, 1923, of being "business-like and progressive and he is frequently remembered as one of the best mayors Williamsport ever had."

LYCOMING COUNTY'S HISTORIAN

There is one person who towers above all others in preserving and recording the history of Lycoming County and the surrounding region: John Franklin Meginness. His books, *The History of Lycoming County* (1892) and *Otzinachson, A History of the West Branch Valley* (1889), withstood the test of time and are the finest reference works for the history of this area.

Born on July 16, 1827 on a farm in Lancaster County, Meginness left home at the age of 16, eventually joining the army for service in the Mexican War. He kept an extensive diary and wrote an unpublished novel, *The Mexican Captive.* After the war, in 1849, he married Martha Jane King of Mifflin Township, and the couple had ten children. They moved to Jersey Shore and Meginness worked for the local newspaper, the *Jersey Shore Republican*. In 1852, he became its editor.

He began writing *Otzinachson*, an Indian name for the Susquehanna River, in 1855, conducting exhaustive research and financing its publication with his money. First published in 1856, he revised and updated a lengthier version in 1889.

He moved to Williamsport and became editor of the *Lycoming Gazette* in 1864. The newspaper merged with another, becoming the *Gazette and Bulletin*, from which Meginness retired in 1889. In 1883, Meginness founded and edited a monthly magazine, *The Historical Journal*, and wrote biographical accounts of many in Lycoming County's history, including one of Frances Slocum, the lost sister of the Wyoming Massacre, in 1891.

The Imperial Teteques Band of the Knights Templar was founded in 1899 and is the oldest Masonic Band in the world. The 1889 Imperial Teteques Band consisted of, from left to right, (front row), Frank Pearson and Fred E. Allen; (middle row) Clarence E. Else, Charles V. Runkle, Lyman J. Fisk, Herbert R. Laird, John K. Hays, and John A. Shoemaker; (back row) William S. Hazelet, Arthur G. Lindley, John H. Watson, William F. Vandersloot, William C. King, T.P. Reitmeyer, Fred Schrutz, and Howard H. Monteling. (LCHS.)

Meginness died on November 11, 1899 at the age of 72. His epitaph reads: "John F. Meginness, Journalist and Historian, 1827–1899. He Labored for Posterity."

THE IMPERIAL TETEQUES BAND

One of the oldest Masonic-sponsored bands in the world—the Imperial Teteques Band—came into existence more than 100 years ago as an organization designed to enliven monthly dinner meetings of Masonic bodies. It was the brainchild of four men and the pampered darling of the fifth.

On a wintry night in November 1894, John King Hays, Herbert Russell Laird, Clarence E. Else, and Truman Purdy Reitmeyer first resolved to start a band in Baldwin II Commandery No. 22, Knights Templar. The Ancient Accepted Scottish Rite had not yet established bodies in Williamsport. These men, each of them destined to become prominent civic and Masonic figures, had limited musical training but boundless enthusiasm for instrumental music. They rented several wind instruments and soon became proficient enough for public performances. They were billed as the Triple Tongue Quartet. From the first letters of these words—TTQ—the band derives its unique name.

J. Walton Bowman became the band's business manager and financial angel, and the band won acclaim wherever the Masons sponsored instrumental music. As Bowman's "pampered darling," the Teteques Band built up a $100,000 inventory of instruments and a vast library of music during the quarter century he served as manager.

Following Bowman's death in 1931, interest in the band diminished, but in 1956, H. Carion Sweeley, a clarinetist, rejuvenated the band and became manager. Since 1963, the band has been sponsored by the Ancient Accepted Scottish Rite in the Valley of Williamsport and is officially known as the Scottish Rite Imperial Teteques. The band plays to an estimated 2,000 persons during its varied concert presentations each season in the Scottish Rite Auditorium.

During the 1999–2000 season, the Scottish Rite Imperial Teteques Band made history again as it admitted female members to its ranks for the first time. That season's first four female members were Dee Dee Hensler, Shelia Hornberger, Donna Speigel, and Sarah Van Auken.

African-Americans formed their own Masonic organizations as typified here by this picture of the local St. John's Black Masonic Band. (LCHS.)

9. New Century, New Ideas

From 1850 through the early 1900s, Williamsport was known as the Lumber Capital of the World. One man who epitomized the era was Christ Haist, who worked at all levels in the lumber industry and helped to create the wealth of the "Lumber Barons."

Born near Linden in 1858, Haist grew up in the Pine Run area. As a young boy, he worked in the lumber business as a "boom rat," or manual laborer, on the Susquehanna Boom. By 1909, he had risen through the ranks of lumber workers to become the last superintendent of the Susquehanna Boom. He was in charge of the boom when the last log, part of a drive coming out of the Pine Creek area, was rafted out on June 8, 1909. When he died on August 16, 1944, an era passed into history.

As the lumber industry declined, many turned to farming. However, there was not enough cleared and available land for all, so many families were obliged to move from the area in their search for employment. For years, business and industry were at a standstill. To prevent Williamsport and its neighboring communities from becoming ghost towns, and to avert financial and industrial collapse, a trade association was formed to attract new industries to the county and revitalize the region in the first half of the twentieth century.

Early historians speculate that during a 20-year period from 1894 to 1914, virtually every aspect of life in Lycoming County communities was affected by sweeping changes. The disastrous floods of 1889 and 1894 were catalysts of change; other changes were propelled by developments in communication and transportation. Extensive unemployment and lower living standards accompanied business panics in 1893 and 1907. Politicians reexamined their beliefs in political and industrial democracy, reflected in the nationwide battle for political supremacy as the Republican Party split, handing the presidential election to Woodrow Wilson.

Locally, there were bitter political discussions and candidates of the Socialist Party would at times receive a substantial number of votes. Also during this period, groups demanded a woman's suffrage amendment to the Constitution, as well as prohibition of alcohol manufacturing and consumption.

Various social activists and crusaders visited Williamsport over the years. One of the most prominent was temperance crusader Carrie Nation. The *Williamsport*

Sun reported on November 8, 1902 that Nation visited the saloons of the city and gave the proprietors a piece of her "lively mind."

Nation lectured before an audience at Association Hall and strolled down the streets the next morning, the center of attention everywhere. The newspaper reported on the event:

> Men jostled each other and women walked squares ahead and sparred for points of vantage and small boys fought for the privilege of getting close to her. Dressed in a sober black gown, with a little bonnet on her head, she passed through the storming throng. In the saloons she walked directly up to the bar, put her right arm on top, and pointing her finger directly at the bartender and she would tell them what she thought without mincing words. She told them, "Do you know sir, that you are in a business that is taking the bread and butter out of the mouths of wives and children of this town? Poor men come in and drink this vile stuff and then go home and beat and abuse their wives and children. God will surely punish such wickedness. You ought to be ashamed of the business and get out of it right away. Why no decent woman would come in here to buy anything and you have no business running a place that a decent woman can't visit. Yes sir, you are going straight to hell, and you had better take warning and quit while you have the time."

During her trip, Nation visited the hotel of M.J. Winters and in the barroom she encountered a corpulent man drinking a glass of beer. She told him of the evils of the thing, and when he made some derogatory remarks in return, she turned to the crowd and said, "Look at him! He looks like a beer keg out on a pair of skates."

"That's all right, I've been in jail, and that's more than you can say," said the man.

Nation shot back, "Yes, I've been to jail, but I got out. But you're going to hell, and you'll never get out."

WILLIAMSPORT'S MUSICAL HERITAGE

One distraction that wasn't outlawed or shunned in Williamsport was music. During the late 1890s and early 1900s, the city was a major music publishing center and Frederick W. Vandersloot owned the largest music publishing company.

A fairly good singer, his piano accompanist failed to show up at an engagement and someone suggested that Cora Elwest accompany him. They performed "I'll Take You Home Again Kathleen." Vandersloot took Cora home and shortly thereafter married her.

Reportedly, Vandersloot became interested in starting a music publishing business because Cora had composed a song titled "Yellow Kids on Parade." He had a number of copies of her song published to give to friends and it soon became popular. John Philip Sousa's band performed Cora's composition at the Lycoming

Opera House on October 7, 1897. It was the only non-Sousa composition played at the concert. She composed another fairly popular march called the "Greater America March" in 1898.

Around that time, Vandersloot founded the Vandersloot Music Publishing Company, supposedly in the kitchen of his Washington Boulevard home. From 1901 through 1902, he lived in New York City to learn more about the music publishing business and to establish contacts. In 1903, he returned and reestablished his business. The company would eventually have branch offices in New York City, Toronto, Chicago, and London.

In 1911, Vandersloot enjoyed his greatest success as a writer and publisher when his song "I Wonder How the Old Folks are at Home" became immensely popular. It is reported to have cleared $85,000 in its first five months of publication. The song enjoyed a revival in popularity during World War I among American doughboys in the trenches of Europe.

His strong religious faith played a role in the type of music he chose. Although his company published a wide catalog, he chose never to publish any jazz because he regarded it to be of dubious morality. An active member of the Pine Street

The Williamsport Opera House was designed by architect Eber Culver. "March King" John Philip Sousa's band performed resident Cora Vandersloot's composition at the Opera House on October 7, 1897. It was the only non-Sousa composition played at the concert. (LCHS.)

Methodist Church, he served as its choir director for 28 years, as well as its steward and a trustee. As a testament to his great religious faith he composed and published "Echoes of Old Pine," a collection of 19 gospel songs. He accepted no royalties for them.

His company was a major outlet for other local composers, including Charles Sweeley, who composed the "Repasz Band March" and Harry J. Lincoln. In 1930, Vandersloot sold his business to Lincoln, who had composed more than 75 marches while living in Williamsport, most published by Vandersloot. Lincoln moved the company to Philadelphia, where it operated until his death in 1937. Vandersloot died on July 30, 1931.

Herbert Laird and the Board of Trade

As the lumber trade faded, Williamsport reorganized the board of trade, the predecessor of today's Williamsport/Lycoming Chamber of Commerce. Its general manager in 1900 was Colonel Herbert R. Laird, also known as the father of the Lycoming County Historical Society.

Laird was a man of diverse abilities and interests, and also one of Williamsport's most tireless business boosters and promoters. Laird worked for the *Williamsport Sun* in various capacities, starting as a reporter and later becoming treasurer. In 1894, he left the newspaper business and entered the fire insurance and real estate business.

His leadership at the board of trade coincided with the lumber trade fading in the area, when the development of replacement industries was desperately needed. He played a key role in the diversification of Williamsport's industrial infrastructure, and when Williamsport celebrated its centennial in 1906, Laird came up with imaginative and spectacular ways to promote the city. He had a billboard erected opposite the popular and busy Bellvue-Stratford Hotel in Philadelphia, touting Williamsport as "The Ideal City for Home and Business."

Under Laird's leadership, the board of trade acted on a plan devised by prominent local attorney C. Larue Munson to establish a guaranty fund that was used to underwrite industrial financing. Area businessmen pledged $215,000 to the fund, which became critical in the board's quest for industries. Laird once said of this fund, "this feature of the Board of Trade was of greater value from a publicity standpoint than from any other, and Williamsport attracted much favorable attention throughout the nation because of it."

Laird had a deep and abiding passion for the area's history and saw the organization of a permanent historical society as an important aid to promoting and advertising the attractions of this area. In 1907, he was instrumental in organizing the society, and in 1940, he helped launch a drive to give the organization and its holdings a permanent home, raising $6,000 by personal subscription towards the purchase of the Maynard mansion at 858 West Fourth Street.

The Lycoming County Centennial Parade is held in Williamsport in 1895 along Market Square looking west on West Third Street. (LCHS.)

THE FLYING MACHINE

Northcentral Pennsylvania has a strong involvement with aviation, with companies such as Lycoming Motors, the forerunner to Textron, and Piper Aircraft in Lock Haven. One of the earliest aviation pioneers here was Harry Burns.

Born on January 1, 1892 in Williamsport, Burns and his brother Fred showed an early interest in gadgetry and were fascinated by Orville and Wilbur Wright's achievement in the first powered flight at Kitty Hawk, North Carolina, on December 17, 1903. By 1910, the Burns brothers and their friend August Kuntz designed and built their own flying machine, a bi-winged glider. It was 25 feet long and had a frame made of light wood covered with strong muslin. The two wings were connected with stout wires that crossed diagonally.

Aviation history in Williamsport began with the flight of the Burns' glider over Grampian Hills on a bright Sunday morning, September 18, 1910. They began the test of their flying machine about 5 a.m. when the brothers climbed into position, and "a gust of wind picked up the glider and passengers, swooshed them down the Grampian incline and deposited them unceremoniously wrong-side up," according to a 1973 interview with Harry Burns.

Unfortunately, that finished the fragile glider, but their brief flight caused quite a stir.

The next day, the *Williamsport Gazette and Bulletin* told of the many wild rumors that spread following the short flight, such as an "airship on its way from Philadelphia to Pittsburgh was forced to land here." Another was that an "aeroplane flying from Elmira to Philadelphia was forced down in the Grampian Hills." Still another said, "A woman was awakened early in the morning by the aeroplane, and it made a noise like a railroad train."

Harry Burns remembered his adventure well, even 63 years after it happened. "Word got out that the aeroplane had landed, which started people coming out. The East End trolley brought so many people we had to take the glider home."

By 1911, they built a monoplane, but they needed a motor. Harry went to work at a bank in Cleveland that year, where he met a man who owned a 25-horsepower Curtiss engine. He traded the monoplane glider for the motor, and the Burns brothers built another plane using a fuselage of spruce wood and a landing gear of white ash, with a wing span of 28 feet, to use with the newly acquired motor. The plane flew up to 60 miles per hour—speedy at that time.

The Burns brothers eventually left Williamsport. Fred went to San Diego to pursue other interests, but Harry stayed in the aviation field. He became an expert in wing covering, making rubberized silk wings for airplanes. His aptitude led him to become a foreman with the Curtiss Engineering Company in Garden City, Long Island, New York, headed by aviation pioneer and early airplane manufacturer Glenn H. Curtiss.

In 1914, Burns flew the Model F aircraft powered by a Curtiss engine. He oversaw the covering of the navy's NC-4 flying boat in 1919, which was one of

Harry Burns was an early aviation pioneer in the Williamsport area. He is seen here with his aeroplane about 1920. (WSG/GRIT.)

the first aircraft to successfully cross the Atlantic, and he was a member of the OX-5 Club, dedicated to commemorating the spirit of the pioneers of aviation. "You had to be a flyer or a Curtiss employee before 1940," Burns said of the club's requirements, both of which he met.

By 1920, Burns decided to leave aviation and join his brother in San Diego, where he lived for a number of years before returning to Williamsport. He died on June 3, 1976 in the United Methodist Home in Lewisburg.

THE AUTOMOBILE

One family, the Bubbs, not only opened the first car dealership in Williamsport, but also was responsible for the only car to be manufactured in the city. In 1905, Nathaniel Burrows Bubb, a prominent businessman, constructed an automobile garage at the corner of West Third and Locust Streets. Two of his sons, Harry and Nathaniel Jr., rented the garage from their father and began the fledgling automobile dealership selling Reo and White cars. In 1906, the Bubbs' dealership had prospered and they decided to manufacture their own automobiles. The prototype called for a two-seat passenger roadster of the semi-racing type, designed by the Exchange's manager, C.P. Van Ferls. The Imperial Roadster was given its first test run on April 2, 1907, reportedly reaching 60 miles per hour with a 35-horsepower engine. In 1908, two Imperials were for sale—a runabout with a folding rumble seat cost $2,500 and a roadster with four seats cost $2,650.

As many as 50 Imperials were manufactured, but the car's engine was underpowered and could not compete in the "touring runs" most car companies used

The standard form of urban transportation in Williamsport from the 1860s until the early 1900s was the horse-drawn passenger trolley before the automobile gained such prominence. (JVBL.)

This sketch is of the 1907 Imperial roadster, the only automobile ever manufactured in Williamsport. The Imperial Motor Car Company went out of business in 1909. (LCHS.)

to promote new models. Also, the financial Panic of 1907 made it difficult for many people to obtain loans, and on September 4, 1908, the company petitioned the court to put the company into receivership and eventual bankruptcy. Thus ended Williamsport's chapter in automobile manufacturing and the dream of the Bubb family.

PHILANTHROPIST J. ROMAN WAY

J. Roman Way probably is best remembered for his philanthropy. He gave generously to the YMCA, the YWCA, and the Williamsport Hospital building funds, and made large cash contributions to the Children's Aid Society and the Home for the Friendless. But perhaps Way's most enduring legacy is the garden that bears his name.

The 2.5-acre plot that became Way's Garden at the southeast corner of West Fourth and Maynard Streets originally contained the mansion of one of the area's leading lumber millionaires, John White. The mansion was such an imposing structure that it was known as "White's Castle." Way and his wife lived in the former Judge Maynard house, which was on the site now supporting Lycoming County Historical Museum. The "castle" was across the street from the Ways.

When John White died in the early 1900s, prospective buyers announced their intention to use the mansion as a boardinghouse. That prospect did not please Way or his wife. Way envisioned a nice garden with attractive plantings rather than the rough hurly-burly of a boardinghouse, so he bought the property and had the "castle" razed, brick-by-brick. In April 1913, Way presented the land permanently to the city as a scenic garden, establishing an endowment for the upkeep of it. A commission was established to supervise the maintenance of the garden.

Auburn cars on parade April 28, 1932 head west on West Third Street near the LL Stearns Department Store and the Lycoming County Courthouse. The Auburn automobile used a Lycoming engine manufactured in Williamsport. (LCHS.)

CLEO PINEAU: DAREDEVIL MOTORCYCLIST, WORLD WAR I ACE

Taking chances provided Cleo Francois Pineau with success in several different arenas. Pineau was a daredevil motorcyclist, a World War I fighter ace, and a successful businessman. Even though he became a well-known businessman in his later years, information on his early years tends to be spotty. He was reportedly born in Albuquerque, New Mexico, on July 23, 1893. His father Thomas Pineau was a Williamsport native and a one-time member of the Williamsport Police Department.

According to his daughter Andree Phillips, Pineau was a very restless youth. He was expelled from several different schools and dropped out in the sixth grade. His love of motion and daring led him to be one of the nation's leading motorcycle racers, using Flying Merkel and Indian brand motorcycles for his racing. In one race, he defeated the famous Barney Oldfield, who was both a motorcycle and car racer and one of the early winners of the Indianapolis 500.

His prowess with a motorcycle also took him on the vaudeville circuit. He performed in something called the "Globe of Death." An ad for it proclaimed, "Vaudeville's Most Sensational Novelty: Tinkham's Globe of Death. A Daredevil, Death-Defying Riding Exhibition, Featuring Cleo Pineau's Thrilling Loop-the-Loop on a Motorcycle Traveling 60 Miles an Hour."

The spirit of adventure overtook him again when World War I came along, and he enlisted in the Royal Canadian Air Force before the United States entered the war. A letter to his mother reads:

> Today I enlisted in the Royal Flying Corps. I have taken up flying at the Curtiss Aviation School at Buffalo. Flying is so much less

Cleo Pineau poses next to his plane and his motorcycle in the years before World War I. He was a noted daredevil motorcycle rider on the motorcycle racing circuit. Some of those tendencies may have helped him as a flyer. A Williamsport resident, he enlisted in the Royal Canadian Air Force and shot down six German planes. He later became president of the Radiant Steel Company in Williamsport. (LCHS.)

> dangerous than motorcycle racing; in fact there is no danger in it at all. I will get a good Commission. It might be well to advise the Draft Officials of Albuquerque that I have enlisted so they can check me off their list.

He was finally posted to a squadron in France in June 1918. He soon distinguished himself in combat in his Sopwith Camel plane, tangling in life-and-death aerial struggles with the "Dreaded Hun" and his Fokker D.VIIs biplanes. He destroyed six enemy planes, placing him in the ace category, but he was shot down on October 8, 1918. Fortunately, he escaped death and serious injury and spent the final five weeks of the war in a German prisoner of war camp, with Kaiser Wilhelm II's son as its commandant.

When he was shot down, his mother received a letter from the British Air Ministry saying he was missing and presumed dead, but he was able to write his mother through the auspices of the Red Cross shortly after his arrival at the prison camp. After his release Pineau was decorated with Britain's Distinguished Flying Cross. The commendation that went with the award read in part, "An officer of exceptional merit, who sets a very high example of courage and devotion to duty to the other pilots." Britain's King George V penned Pineau a letter in his own hand welcoming his safe release from the camp. The letter reads in part, "The Queen joins me in welcoming you on your release from the miseries and hardships which you have endured with so much patience and courage. During these many months of trial, the early rescue of our gallant officers and men from

A group of Williamsporters celebrate Armistice Day, November 11, 1918, on a wagon proclaiming "The Kaiser Going to Hell." (JVBL.)

Soldiers of the local Battery D of the Pennsylvania National Guard leave for World War I duty in the spring of 1918. (LCHS.)

the cruelties of their captivity has been uppermost in our thoughts." Pineau also received the British War Medal and the Franco-Belgian War Medal.

After the war, he came to Williamsport and, with the help of the investment of some prominent businessmen, founded the Radiant Steel Products Company, which continues today as a successful business under the able stewardship of his daughter. His interest in aviation and its future for commerce prompted him to help in the effort to build the Williamsport-Lycoming County Airport (now the Williamsport Regional Airport) in 1929. His acquaintance with some of the leading aviators of the era prompted the attendance at the airport's opening by figures such as Amelia Earhart.

Pineau also was instrumental in the founding of the West Branch Manufacturers Association in the 1930s, a trade association helping to advance the needs and interests of the area's manufacturing businesses. He was the treasurer of the group for more than 20 years and an honorary life director. In his older years, he still flirted with speed in his boat, and was a founder and first commodore of the West Branch Motorboat Club. His interesting and eventful life came to a quiet end on May 29, 1972.

WILLIAMSPORT'S SUFFRAGE STRUGGLE

The campaign to gain women the vote was a major and hotly contested social issue from the 1840s until the passage of the 19th Amendment in 1919. The first and largest suffrage rally in the Williamsport occurred on March 19, 1914; the

A shopkeeper poses inside his cigar factory on Washington Boulevard in Williamsport. There were many small manufacturing businesses in the area during the late nineteenth and early twentieth centuries. (JVBL.)

Lycoming County courthouse was packed as advocates gathered to speak. The ushers and others brought up more chairs, and they were quickly seized. People sat on window ledges, on the steps to the judge's bench, the steps of the jury box, wherever there was room, while scores stood at the rear and around the sides.

The speakers included Dr. Sophonisba Breckenridge of Chicago, Illinois, a member of the faculty of Chicago University. The other speakers were the state secretary of the Suffrage League, Miss Hall, Dr. Elliot C. Armstrong, pastor of the Central Presbyterian Church, and Julia Smith, president of the state Rural Progress Association.

Elizabeth Crocker presided as chairman and welcomed the people, expressing her gratitude to those who helped make the meeting successful. She told how a few years earlier no one would care to be called a suffragette, but by then things had changed. Armstrong spoke briefly and told how he has always stood for equal suffrage and how he has watched the favorable growth of sentiment for women's votes, speaking of the evening as a historic one, since it was the first mass meeting for equal suffrage ever held in Williamsport. He told those in attendance that he believed the Bible justified suffrage for women.

An editorial in the *Gazette and Bulletin* on the same day also supported the meeting's aim:

> We can scarcely conceive of the necessity in this country of the methods used in England by suffragettes to obtain their desires or draw attention to their cause. The average American is unable to understand all the turmoil there, and the reason we apprehend is the feeling that it is a right the women should be accorded for the asking. The record made up from the states permitting female suffrage, some of them for many years, indicates no ill effects flowing from the extension to them of their rights, but on the contrary all the indications point to the benefit to the body politic, as well as social, from the extension of the franchise.

THE PERSON FAMILY: CIVIC SERVICE AND JOURNALISM

A Williamsport family that typifies civic service and journalism is the Persons. Elmer Person, born in Aristes in 1865, worked as a breaker boy at a coal mine near Centralia late in the nineteenth century. His mother died when he was 15 and he lived with an older sister in Bloomsburg where he learned the printer's trade.

Women's suffragists march for the right to vote in a parade on West Fourth Street in 1913. (LCHS.)

He moved to Williamsport and worked for several different newspapers as a printer, then turned his attention to reporting while at the *Sun and Banner*. He moved to the *Pennsylvania Grit* and eventually became the city editor. In 1900, he accepted the city editorship of the *Williamsport Sun* and, in 1906, he became the paper's editor. In 1912, he died at the age of 47.

His son John E. Person followed his father into the newspaper profession, first working as a part-time reporter during his high school days and then returning full time after his father's death. He became an editor in 1918.

In 1926, George G. Graff, owner of the *Sun* newspaper, acquired the *Gazette and Bulletin*, forming the Sun-Gazette Company. John Person became executive editor of the *Sun* newspaper in 1926 and general manager of both newspapers in 1932. After Graff's death in 1935, Person became the president of the Sun-Gazette Company.

Throughout the years, Person earned the respect of the journalistic community on a national level as he rose to high councils of the Fourth Estate. He served for a time as president of the Pennsylvania Newspaper Publishers Association and the president of the Pennsylvania Members of the Associated Press. He also helped develop the journalism curriculum at Penn State University.

The Williamsport Sun *newspaper often would post breaking news on its Fourth Street wall for passersby to browse. (WSG/GRIT.)*

John Person became executive editor of the Sun *newspaper in 1926 and general manager of both the* Sun *and the* Gazette *in 1932. After owner George G. Graff's death in 1935, Person became the president of the Sun-Gazette Company. (WSG/ GRIT.)*

Civic activism also was important, and he directed a relief shelter for refugees during the 1936 flood and was a strong advocate for a comprehensive flood-warning system. He was an officer or director of nearly three dozen community organizations and raised more than $2 million as chairman of various fundraising drives. *The Grit* gave him its Community Service Award in 1939, an award his son John E. Person Jr. also later received. He died on March 18, 1967.

John "Jack" Person Jr. followed his father into the newspaper business, and continued his family's tradition of improving the community. After attending Dickinson College in Carlisle and the Rochester Institute of Technology and spending four years in the army during World War II, John Jr. returned to Williamsport to work in the national advertising division of the newspaper.

He succeeded his father as president of the company in 1964. Like his father and grandfather before him, he is an active member of the Pine Street Church and has served in several civic organizations. In the late 1950s, Person led a successful effort on the part of local businesses and organizations to keep Little League Baseball's headquarters in Lycoming County when it was considering a move to New York City. He retired from the newspaper profession in 1990 when the Sun-Gazette Company was sold to Ogden Newspapers of West Virginia.

10. The Rise of Recreation

From the 1890s through the early 1950s, D. Vincent Smith was a familiar sight throughout northcentral Pennsylvania with his box camera and heavy-duty bicycle, wearing knickers, sneakers, and scoop cap. He left behind a priceless photographic heritage.

Smith was born on July 24, 1875 in the Nippenose Valley, the son of James W. and Mathilda Homer Smith. It is unknown what prompted his deep and abiding interest in photography, which brought him widespread fame throughout the state. He specialized in rural scenes and portrait work among rural residents, photographing hundreds of sites and buildings that no longer exist.

Smith never owned a car. For 62 years, he pedaled more than 150,000 miles, taking more than 33,000 photographs. One summer he used a horse and buggy, but returned to his bicycle because he could "never make good time" with the buggy. More than any other man, he probably knew Lycoming County best. It was said you could name a corner and he could tell you what previously occupied the site. It was likely he could mentally reach back into his rich collection of photographic plates and negatives to summon up an image of the place.

His images showed business activities such as the building of the Lycoming County Airport, or logging and ice cutting on the Susquehanna, and occasions like festivals and parades. A resident of South Williamsport for more than 60 years, he kept many of his photographic plates and negatives in the basement of his home. He died on July 20, 1955, just four days short of his 80th birthday. His storehouse of photos is preserved at the Lycoming County Historical Museum.

George Fleming and the YMCA

The rise and development of the YMCA, recreation, and physical education in this city in the twentieth century are credited to George R. Fleming. Fleming came to work at the YMCA in Williamsport in 1908. Almost immediately, he demonstrated his innovation and resourcefulness, establishing the first municipally run and supervised playground in this city. At about the same time, he pioneered the concept of physical education, establishing a period during each school day for gym classes. Those classes combined various types of sports and physical culture, including calisthenics. He introduced the game of soccer to this city in 1911.

Fleming had an abiding interest in the moral and physical improvement of young people. Perhaps that is why he organized the first Boy Scout troop in this city at the "Y," Troop 1 in 1910. His work for the YMCA, as its assistant physical education director, finally yielded dividends for him when he was named the general secretary of the local YMCA in 1937. In 1908, the YMCA had a membership of 500, but when he retired in 1948, it was more than 3,000.

During his tenure he oversaw several expansions of its programs and helped to shepherd its growth as a major recreational institution in the area. Basketball teams under his leadership won five YMCA state titles, and the 1937 team also won the international title by defeating Jersey City, New Jersey, 28–27.

Regarded for years as an outstanding leader in physical education work and later in general YMCA administration, Fleming was also physical training director for the 28th Division of the Pennsylvania National Guard and went overseas with them during World War I. His 88 full years of life ended on September 20, 1972.

D. Vincent Smith, the bicycling photographer, often rode his bicycle to a photo shoot. He captured thousands of images of the Williamsport area from the 1890s to the 1950s. (LCHS.)

BOWER'S BASKETBALL FOR YOUTH

For more than 40 years, in his capacity as a juvenile probation officer and as the organizer of two major sports programs, John H. Bower helped keep perhaps thousands of idle boys out of trouble.

As a youth he was an ardent participant in various sandlot sports, including baseball and basketball. From 1907 to 1917, he played in the City League basketball teams at the YMCA. His play with the Y team was parlayed into permanent employment in 1911 when he became assistant secretary there. In 1914, he moved to Rochester, New York to work at Eastman Kodak, spending five years there and playing on the company basketball team that competed against some of the best semi-pro basketball teams in the East, including the famous Buffalo Germans, one of the all-time best amateur basketball squads.

After returning to Williamsport in 1919, he became the boy's work secretary at the YMCA, where two years later he organized the basketball league that bears his name. The league recently celebrated its 80th anniversary season and is the oldest Sunday school basketball league in the world. One of the features of the league

This bird's-eye view of Williamsport is from Bald Eagle Mountain looking north across the Susquehanna River. This photograph was taken by one of Williamsport's most prolific photographers, D. Vincent Smith. (LCHS.)

This photo from the late 1860s is the earliest known image of a baseball team in Williamsport, a town known throughout the world because of Little League Baseball. (JVBL.)

that continues to this day is the rule that players must submit written proof of attendance at Sunday school. He saw the firm moral education of Sunday school as a way to set a firm base for responsible and law-abiding men. That same year, he organized a Sunday school baseball league that existed until 1940 and was a forerunner for the Little League Baseball program.

Bower was an early and enthusiastic leader in the Boy Scouts, helping to form one of the first troops at the YMCA in 1919, using the camping area known later as Camp Kline. In 1925, he set up one of the first attempts at vocational education in the area with a program called "Move Up Forward," in which high school seniors received vocational counseling by some of the city's industrial, civic, and business leaders.

Bower organized the first "Knothole Gang" for baseball-minded youngsters to enjoy Williamsport Grays' games at Bowman Field, helping to develop a lifelong interest in baseball for many youngsters. County officials recognized his magic touch with youth, and in 1941, judges Don Larrabee and Samuel Humes appointed him the county's chief juvenile probation officer. His approach to his job is best epitomized by a quote he always took to heart: "it is easier to train boys than to mend boys." He also was a firm adherent to the view that there are "no bad boys."

Bower died on October 16, 1962, a day after he turned 72. The West Branch Valley Sports Hall of Fame posthumously honored him with induction in 1977.

THE WILLIAMSPORT GRAYS AND THE CITY'S LOVE AFFAIR WITH BASEBALL

In addition to basketball, Williamsport has had a long-lasting love affair with baseball, and for nearly 40 years, the city's professional baseball team was called the Williamsport Grays, named for Thomas M. Gray.

When Gray's uncle Harvey Milnor became Lycoming County sheriff in 1902, he was appointed as a deputy sheriff and, in 1919, was elected sheriff. Gray's tenure, according to contemporaries, was marked with honest, fair, and efficient administration of the office. He also was prominent in political and fraternal circles, serving as one of Lycoming County's representatives on the Republican State Committee and being active on the county's Republican committee.

Gray is best remembered, however, for his involvement in Williamsport's professional baseball scene, serving from 1904 until 1910 as secretary-treasurer of the city's Tri-State League team. Under his administration, Williamsport gained as one of the best operated (if over-financed) professional clubs in the league. Williamsport teams won Tri-State League championships in 1905, 1907, and 1908.

Gray was the prime mover when Williamsport rejoined professional baseball in 1923 as a charter member of the New York-Pennsylvania League (later the Eastern

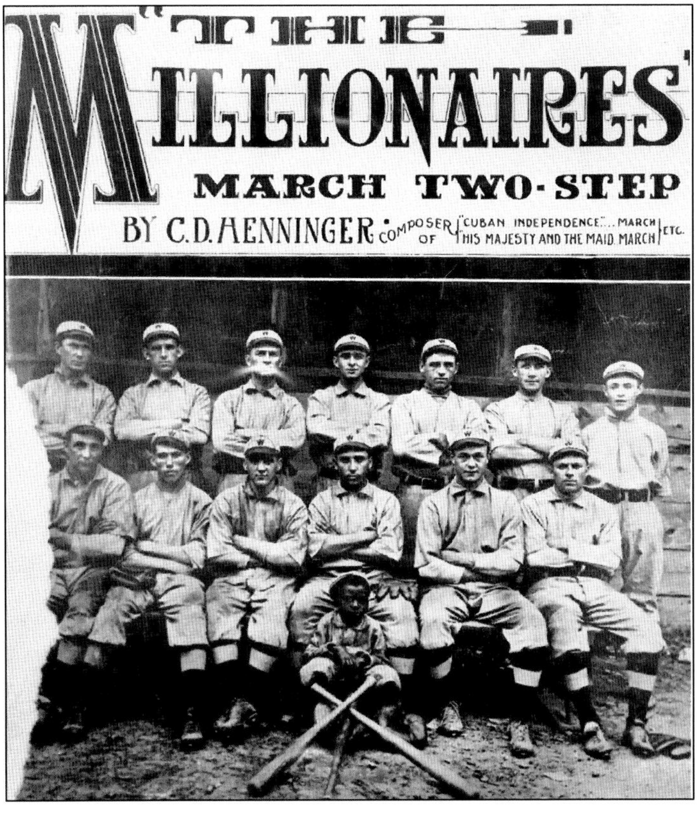

"The Millionaires March," a musical piece by C.D. Henninger, was commissioned to celebrate Williamsport's baseball championship in the professional Tri-State League in 1908. (JVBL.)

League). He also became the secretary-treasurer of that team. Unfortunately, he would not live to see the team win the league's first championship. On August 29, 1923, he died of a massive heart attack.

Gray was posthumously honored in 1924 when the *Gazette and Bulletin* conducted a contest to rename the Williamsport baseball club. Jess Gilbert's entry was determined to be the most appropriate when he suggested the team be named the "Grays" in honor of the late sheriff, who did so much for baseball in Williamsport. That name survived with several minor exceptions until 1962.

NAMESAKE OF BOWMAN FIELD

A historical marker at Bowman Field commemorates Pennsylvania's oldest minor league ballpark and America's second oldest one. Bowman Field was named for J. Walton Bowman, born on February 16, 1864 in Clearfield County, the son of Benjamin C. and Eliza Ann Buck Bowman. Benjamin Bowman was a prominent lumber dealer and manufacturer.

J. Walton Bowman was educated in the private schools of Williamsport and graduated from Dickinson Seminary (later Lycoming College), after which he helped manage his father's lumber business as the company's vice president. He became extensively involved in banking and finance as director of the Susquehanna Trust Company, a bank his father helped to found. He later became secretary-treasurer of the Rowland Land Company and served as president of Kline and Company hardware dealers. Bowman gained a reputation as one of the leading lumber and coal moguls in Lycoming County. Bowman married Harriet Elizabeth Geiger on October 14, 1886 and they had one daughter, Helen Eliza.

He organized, managed, and helped finance the Imperial Teteques Band, one of the great passions of his life. He also had the distinction of owning the first automobile in Williamsport in 1899, but he is most remembered for his involvement in the local professional baseball scene. When Williamsport joined the Tri-State League in 1904, Bowman and his brother Frank were two of the major financial backers for the team. Their capital, as well as that provided by other Williamsport financiers, enabled the local team to obtain some of the best baseball players available, making the local team one of the best professional baseball teams outside of the major leagues from 1904 to 1910.

When Williamsport returned to professional baseball in 1923 with the advent of the New York-Pennsylvania League, Bowman again was a major "financial angel" for the club. In 1925, he led the fundraising effort to build a new ballpark for the professional team. The ballpark opened the following year.

Bowman became president of the Williamsport Grays ball club in 1926 upon the death of Allen P. Perley, and remained so until his own death five years later. In recognition of Bowman's extensive efforts on behalf of baseball in Williamsport, city and Grays' officials decided to name the ballpark Bowman Field in June 1929.

The Williamsport Grays' top brass, from left to right, are: Grays manager, Glenn Killinger; Grays President J. Walton Bowman; and business manager, J. Roy Clunk on April 13, 1930 at Bowman Field. (JVBL.)

Bowman suffered a heart attack and died on February 14, 1931 after his car slid off the Old Montoursville Road, became stuck, and he attempted to shovel it free.

TOMMY RICHARDSON—THE SHOWMAN

One of Williamsport's most recognized citizens and professional baseball fans for many years was Thomas "Tommy" Richardson. An executive of the Williamsport Grays, he served as president of the Eastern League for 26 years and president of the International League for four. Richardson helped to make Williamsport and its baseball teams widely known throughout the country.

The man known variously as the "Merry Minstrel of Baseball," the "Ambassador of Sunshine," "Torrid Tommy," and the "Man of a Million Wisecracks" was born on May 3, 1895, the son of a poor, working-class family of Irish descent. He had to quit school while in the seventh grade when his father died. Richardson once told the *Sun-Gazette*, "I had four jobs and made $8 a week out of all of them. I was so poor my family invented the open-toed shoe."

Richardson and his brother Joe got into show business on the vaudeville circuit where they were known as a song-and-dance team. After his vaudeville days and a tour in the navy during World War I, he returned to Williamsport, eventually owning and operating a Buick dealership for more than 30 years. His show business talent helped him become a professional and entertaining after-dinner speaker and toastmaster. In the words of the writer L.H. Addington, "No baseball banquet was complete without the little imp of fun spouting his saucy stuff from the dais."

Baseball beckoned for Richardson in the early 1920s when he became one of the directors of the Williamsport Grays, rising later to vice president of the club. It was in this capacity that he became a close friend of the legendary Connie Mack of the Philadelphia Athletics. Mack placed Richardson on the A's payroll for three years as a goodwill ambassador. When the great A's team of 1929 to 1931 went to the World Series, it was Tommy and his brother Joe who kept the players loose and relaxed with riotous stories during the rigors of the games.

Richardson's warm relationship with Mack produced positive dividends for both the Williamsport ballclub and Richardson. Beginning in 1931 and off-and-on through 1953, the A's would play the Grays in exhibition games at Bowman Field. Additionally, from 1933 to 1942 and again in 1953, the Grays had a formal working agreement with the A's in which they would stock the Grays with players and buy players when needed.

Richardson's friendship with Mack and his good work for the Grays may have been responsible for his election as president of the Eastern League in 1937. Richardson's showmanship helped the league draw 1 million fans for the first time in 1939. He would stage unique events such as dropping a ball from an airplane as part of first ball ceremonies and offering a President's Cup trophy to the team with the highest opening-day attendance. His promotional skills helped make the Eastern League one of only ten minor league circuits to operate during the difficult days of World War II.

Richardson was an early supporter of Little League Baseball during its fledgling years, sponsoring a team for many years at Original Little League. His talents as a showman led Little League to use him as a master of ceremonies in several of the early Little League Baseball World Series tournaments.

A Tri-State League baseball game is in progress at Athletic Park about 1907. Athletic Park served as the home for Williamsport's professional and semi-professional baseball teams from 1890 to 1911. Collegiate and high school football games also were held there. (JVBL.)

Richardson became president of the International League in 1961, succeeding the legendary Frank "Shag" Shaughnessy. He ran the league with the same firm hand he used in the Eastern League, recalling how he dealt with controversy: "I didn't run away from those fights often. I learned to fight early. The neighborhood I came from was so tough if you saw a cat with a tail you knew he had to be a visitor."

Richardson's lavish, jaunty lifestyle had a cost. His philosophy, "If you couldn't be a millionaire, you could at least act like one," had unfortunate consequences. By his death on November 13, 1970, he was practically broke.

Richardson was inducted into the West Branch Sports Hall of Fame in 1975 and was recognized by the National Baseball Hall of Fame in Cooperstown, New York, where there is an exhibit dealing with minor league baseball and its leading players and executives.

SOL "WOODY" WOLF: RADIO MAN

One of the most influential sports figures of the West Branch Valley during most of the twentieth century was Sol "Woody" Wolf. Born in Johannesburg, South Africa, on January 7, 1897, he was the son of Salle and Sarah Friedberg Wolf. The family immigrated to Germany following the death of his father during the Boer War and Wolf attended military school there.

In 1907, his family again moved, this time to the United States, settling in Detroit, Michigan. After two years at the University of Michigan, where Wolf played football, he joined the army and saw action during the Mexican Border Campaign in 1916 against Pancho Villa, and he was in France during World War I.

After the war, he attended the American College of Physical Education, now DePaul University, and attended football-coaching clinics conducted by Knute Rockne and Lou Little. These activities laid an excellent foundation for his coaching career, including stints at Lock Haven and Williamsport High Schools, as well as Lock Haven State College. His Lock Haven High team won the state high school football championship in 1924 and the national championship in 1925.

Wolf was hired by Williamsport to revive the city's nearly moribund high school football team. In five years, he compiled a spectacular 52-2-3 record. In 1927, 1929, and 1930, his teams went undefeated. Local sportswriters dubbed the 1930 team, which piled up 474 points while surrendering only 9, "The Wolfmen."

After retiring from coaching, Wolf worked as a broadcaster, announcing the Williamsport Grays Eastern League baseball games, as well as professional football games. As the voice of the Grays in 1938, he helped inspire Carl Stotz's nephews to want to play baseball in "real uniforms, using real bats and balls," prompting the founding of Little League Baseball. The Pennsylvania Sports Hall of Fame enshrined Wolf in 1973 and he was founder of its West Branch chapter. He died at the age of 90 on August 8, 1987.

A group of youthful baseball players parade in downtown Williamsport in 1930. By the end of the 1930s, organized youth baseball would begin in Williamsport with the advent of Little League Baseball. (WSG/GRIT.)

CARL STOTZ INTRODUCES THE WORLD TO LITTLE LEAGUE

In 1939, a persistent and optimistic 29-year-old Carl E. Stotz had a vision of baseball for boys. He could have no inkling that his modest proposal would become a worldwide youth sports phenomenon that would involve more than 30 million children in more than 100 countries across the globe.

Carl Edwin "Uncle Tuck" Stotz was born in Williamsport on February 20, 1910. He learned the value and dignity of hard work from his father John, who was employed by the Pennsylvania Railroad. He had only modest baseball talent, but still dreamed of playing professional ball. Instead, he played on his church's baseball team in the area Sunday School League.

As an adult, a fateful game of catch and a collision with a lilac bush in the spring of 1938 started Stotz down the path of baseball immortality. He was playing catch with his nephews Jimmy and "Major" Gehron when he stepped on a cut-back lilac bush at the rear of his house at 1108 Isabella Street. Stotz sat down on his back steps tending to his scraped ankle when his nephews joined him and started talking baseball. Stotz later recalled, "I asked my nephews, 'How would you like to play on a regular team with uniforms, a new ball for every game and bats you could really swing?' And they said, 'Will people come to watch us? Do you think a band will ever come to play?' " The boys' enthusiasm also was fired by Sol "Woody" Wolf's radio broadcasts of the Williamsport Grays' professional games from Bowman Field.

Throughout the winter of 1938 and 1939, Stotz was turned down by 56 businesses while searching for sponsors for the new league. Finally, in March 1939, Lycoming Dairy became the first sponsor of a Little League team, providing enough money to order supplies. There was only enough money for one set of catching equipment and the Little League's first three teams shared that equipment. Stotz said for 34¢ he got enough white duck canvas to make two bases, and his sister Lulabelle stitched them up and made them like an envelope. They were filled with excelsior, wood shavings used as packing material by a local drugstore.

Stotz first asked friend Ollie Fawcett to manage one of the teams. Fawcett, however, had to work his victory garden, a patch of land down by the Susquehanna River given to him by the federal government to raise vegetables during the Depression, and could not spare the time. Next, he asked George and Bert Bebble to manage the other two teams that first year (Jumbo Pretzel and Lundy Lumber). The Bebbles asked him not to schedule any games on Wednesdays or Saturdays because they were players in the Central League, a very competitive amateur

The first Little League Baseball team, Lycoming Dairy, was managed by Carl Stotz, founder of Little League. Consisting of three teams managed by Stotz and brothers George and Bert Bebble, Little League played its first game June 6, 1939. A half-century later, there were nearly 200,000 teams worldwide. (LLB.)

baseball circuit of that time. The three men's wives were recruited as volunteers as well.

From this humble, acorn-like beginning, the mighty oak of Little League Baseball was born. World War II slowed the growth of the program, but after the war, Stotz traveled around the country to spread the Little League message. In 1947, the first Little League World Series was played, although it was composed of teams only from Pennsylvania and New Jersey. Stotz was honored with the *Grit*'s Community Service Award in 1948 for his "vision, zeal and continuing efforts on behalf of boys culminating in national acceptance of Little League."

In 1949, Stotz sought corporate sponsorship to help defray the costs of the Little League program. He found a willing national sponsor in U.S. Rubber, maker of Keds sneakers and rubber-cleated baseball shoes for Little Leaguers. Stotz was named Little League's first commissioner and was paid by the rubber company, but the relationship would come back to haunt him.

In 1953, U.S. Rubber brought in Peter J. McGovern to help administer Little League's affairs, but his personality clashed with Stotz's, and the board of directors mostly supported McGovern's positions. Stotz was concerned about the growing commercialization of his brainchild and the composition of the organization's governing board. In 1955, Stotz sued Little League to regain control of the organization and a messy court fight followed, ending with Stotz severing ties with the institution he founded.

Stotz and his loyalists retreated to the Original Little League, but were forbidden by court order from referring to it as "Little" League, and Original League remains outside of Little League Baseball's governance today. Several attempts to bring the two sides together failed, and Stotz never attended a Little League Baseball World Series after 1955, although he did enjoy attending his grandchildren's Little League games.

Stotz was honored for his contributions to the youth of the world by the Freedom Foundation in Valley Forge and the Williamsport Rotary Club, and was inducted in both the West Branch and Pennsylvania State Sports Halls of Fame.

Stotz died on June 5, 1992 at the age of 82. His death was widely mourned and Mayor Phillip E. Preziosi ordered all flags on city buildings to fly at half-staff as a measure of respect for a man whose impact spread far beyond this city. The *Williamsport Sun-Gazette* editorialized on Stotz's death:

> Stotz built a field of dreams here long before Hollywood popularized the phrase in a movie. He was one of the last great folk heroes of our time, a wonderfully golden presence that defined the goodness of the human spirit. His legacy will be that he cared, that a guy from down the street who is committed to a worthwhile goal could start a neighborhood campaign that eventually makes a difference in an uncaring world. And we thank him for the millions of children who have benefited physically and spiritually from his vision.

At Stotz's funeral, his pastor, the Reverend Frank Showers of the Church of Savior Lutheran, compared Stotz to a "modern-day prophet." He cited the prophet-like traits he possessed: "First, he was faithful to the truth. Second, he was a servant of the people, and third, he was man of vision."

Today, Little League Baseball awards funds toward higher education in Carl Stotz's name to deserving high school seniors in Lycoming County. The story of his founding of the Little League program is detailed with an exhibit in the Peter J. McGovern Little League Museum in South Williamsport, and a statue of him now stands at the complex where the annual Little League Baseball World Series is played.

WILLIAMSPORT'S "SUNRAY": RAY KEYES

The man who dominated the sports scene in northcentral Pennsylvania was neither an athlete nor a sports executive but a sportswriter. Although Ray Keyes's name has been linked with Williamsport and its environs for more than 50 years, Keyes was born in Canandagiua, New York, on November 16, 1916. He moved to the Williamsport area with his parents and after graduating from Williamsport High School, worked for Williamsport's morning newspaper, the *Gazette and Bulletin*, in 1937. He had variety of duties, including a stint on the social desk

Hoboes, a regular sight in Williamsport because of easy access to railroad train cars, cook scrounged food near a Williamsport area bridge in December 1931, during the dark days of the Depression. (WSG/GRIT.)

and at one time acting as news editor, but his real love was sports. An early Little League Baseball supporter in 1939, he covered Carl Stotz's fledgling Little League program. He remained a tireless promoter and champion of Little League Baseball for the rest of his life, covering every Little League World Series as official scorer from 1947 through 1988. In 1987, he was honored by Little League with the inaugural W. Howard Hartman Friendship Award for his "proficiency of using the written word to promote Little League."

"His contributions to his community and to Little League were monumental," said Dr. Creighton Hale, former president of Little League Baseball. Longtime sports booster Bill Pickelner echoed these sentiments. "Ray loved Little League. He was always 1,001 percent for it." In 1988, the press box at Howard J. Lamade Stadium, home of the Little League World Series, was named in Keyes's honor.

Keyes served in the Army Air Force in the South Asian Theater in World War II, after which he plunged headlong back into the newspaper business. Some of his fondest times were spent in the press box at Bowman Field covering Williamsport's minor league baseball teams. He was a familiar and friendly face in press boxes throughout the major and minor leagues, reflected in his membership in the Baseball Writers Association of America. He was a major force in assisting in the acquisition of minor league franchises for Williamsport through his extensive baseball contacts, and served as a member of the Bowman Field Commission. Keyes was active in all the Masonic bodies and several civic organizations.

After a courageous battle with cancer, Keyes's prolific pen was stilled on December 11, 1988.

P.D. MITCHELL: A BROTHER TO ALL

Percy D. Mitchell, a man with a broad smile and an even broader sense of community service, served as an inspiration to the African-American community in Williamsport. Mitchell was born in Portsmouth, Virginia, on June 26, 1909, a son of John Wesley and Lollie Mitchell. He was raised in North Carolina and graduated from Johnson Smith College in Charlotte, teaching for 14 years in that state.

In 1943, he came to Williamsport as director of the Bethune-Douglass Community Center, holding that post for the next 33 years. Mitchell had an avid interest in sports as he organized and coached many basketball, baseball, and football teams at Bethune-Douglass. He also coached the first African-American men and women's bowling teams in the county to be recognized by the American Bowling Congress and the Women's International Bowling Congress. He was involved in numerous civic and service organizations, and he was elected the first African-American state governor of the Kiwanis Club, only the second Williamsport member elected to that position. The local chapter of the National Conference of Christians and Jews honored him twice for community service, and he received the *Grit*'s Meritorious Service Award in 1976. He was inducted into the West Branch Sports Hall of Fame in 1980.

One of Mitchell's prime causes was the struggle for racial equality, and although younger African Americans during the 1960s sometimes criticized him for not being more aggressive, Mitchell thought he could be more effective working quietly behind the scenes. He often was successful with that strategy. He was the co-founder of the West Branch Plan for Equality and a member of the Pennsylvania Board of Governors of the State Colleges and Universities.

Mitchell and his wife Amelia had four children. He died on November 10, 1981. Carl R. Andrews, a native Williamsporter and one-time national director of Boys Clubs of America, said of Mitchell, "He is a father to some and a brother to all."

Prominent Williamsport African-American community leader and activist P.D. Mitchell instructs children in the finer points of basketball at the Bethune-Douglass Community Center in the late 1940s. (WSG/GRIT.)

11. The Changing World

Williamsport has enjoyed a colorful history, replete with heroes and villains. Many of its residents have contributed positively to the community, while a few simply entertained. From far-sighted college presidents and musical mayors, to bootleggers and suicidal science fiction writers, Williamsport often seems to be a mirror, reflecting the whims and woes of the nation.

Perhaps, if the city had not been anchored in a lush valley along the West Branch of the Susquehanna, it would have died on the vine at the close of the lumber era. But rich in history, tradition, and diversity, residents of twentieth-century Williamsport could still appreciate culture and technology and never be away from the mountains or the river.

The Transformation of Lycoming College

Perhaps no other person is more identified with the growth and transformation of Lycoming College from a small junior college to a nationally respected and accredited four-year college than Dr. John W. Long. His academic and clerical credentials prompted officials of the Methodist church to name him as president of the then Dickinson Seminary in 1921. In the next 34 years, he would leave an imprint on the college that remains today.

At the time Long became its president, Dickinson Seminary had only three buildings on campus; by the time he left, seven more buildings were constructed that added greatly to the college's facilities and its capacity for academic development. Additionally, Long was generous in granting access to these facilities for the greater good of the community. When the United States entered World War II, Long and officials at Dickinson immediately made plans for the college to assist in the war effort by organizing an army education unit, and a Civil Pilot Cadet training program was started with 110 men enrolled. Army Aviation Cadets and the Cadet Nurse Corps also used the buildings for training. Before Little League Baseball built its own housing facilities, Long allowed the use of the college's dormitories for players coming to Williamsport for the annual World Series.

With the end of World War II, Long saw there were many returning veterans seeking a college education through the benefits granted by the G.I. Bill of Rights.

There were no four-year colleges in the greater Williamsport area and Long thought the conversion of Dickinson into a four-year college would fill the need. He was met with some initial skepticism for his proposal, but he was able to win over the skeptics. On May 8, 1947, Dickinson became Lycoming College.

Long retired as president of Lycoming College on June 30, 1955. During his tenure, enrollment doubled as the college transformed from primarily a Methodist school into one that attracted and nurtured students of all religious denominations. Long died on May 5, 1956 at the age of 73.

LYCOMING'S FIRST WOMAN LEGAL ADVOCATE

Women have been practicing law in various parts of this country from about the mid-nineteenth century on. Lycoming County did not have its first woman legal advocate until 1923: the remarkable Louise Larzelere Chatham.

Chatham had an early passion for the study of the law. After studying for and passing the preliminary Pennsylvania examinations, she entered the Boston University Law School in 1920. She graduated in June 1923 with highest honors and was admitted to practice law in Lycoming County later that year as the first woman to practice law in the county. She was admitted to practice before the Pennsylvania Supreme Court in 1924.

Republican politicos and supporters listen to political speeches at the Lycoming County Republican summer picnic at Sunset Park sometime in the mid-1930s. (WSG/GRIT.)

Bathers cool off at a Lycoming Creek swimming spot at Memorial Park sometime during the 1920s or 1930s. Onlookers watch the fun from the wooden bridge that once spanned the creek. (LCHS.)

Before her involvement in law studies, Louise Chatham was very involved in the church and civic affairs of the area. She was active in the political realm as well, as the first woman vice chairman of the Lycoming County Republican Committee. As the result of her extensive involvement in civic and political affairs, she was appointed to the State Welfare Commission in 1924, serving until 1927. In the words of Thomas Lloyd's *History of Lycoming County*:

> Mrs. Chatham attributes her success in life to persistency and the determination to do her best in all work that she may undertake, regardless of its importance. Her husband's interest in her professional career, as well as her musical and club work, has served as her greatest inspiration throughout the years.

Her beloved husband Newton died suddenly in 1933, and she remained active until her own death on November 13, 1938. In an editorial on November 20, 1938 titled "A Public Spirited Citizen," the *Grit* said the following of Chatham:

> By the death of Louise L. Chatham this city lost a public spirited citizen. The city's first woman lawyer, she used her professional advantage to

> render service to her fellow citizens. She became the moving spirit in the civic club, conceived the idea of Memorial Park and energetically carried out that idea as a further tribute to the boys who went "over there," she secured the renaming of Erie Avenue to Memorial Avenue. She interested herself in scores of questions and activities involving the poor people to whom she generously gave legal service. Mrs. Chatham was a consistent advocate of a "square deal" for everyone.

THE RISE OF STROEHMANN BROTHERS BAKERY

One of the most notable and enduring businesses associated with Williamsport is the Stroehmann Brothers Bakery. Thousands of people in the area grew up with their bread and bakery products, and hundreds of others made a living working at one of the Stroehmann plants.

Carl F. Stroehmann founded Stroehmann Brothers Bakery with his brother Harold. Both were born in Wheeling, West Virginia, the sons of Frederick G. and Louisa Frederika Koehler Stroehmann. Their interest in baking came naturally since their father operated two bakeries in West Virginia and in Ashland, Kentucky. In early 1924, Carl and Harold heard of a bakery for sale here in Williamsport and acquired the Gramlich Bakery for $165,000 plus the inventory.

Among their earliest moves after buying the bakery was membership in a bakery cooperative called Quality Bakers of America. The group was helpful in offering advice and information on the newest innovations in the baking industry. It was through their contact with "QB" that they bought a new high-speed mixer, along with several other state-of-the-art pieces of equipment—the type of equipment and innovations that their local competitors did not have. The relationship with Quality Bakers gave the Stroehmann Brothers a marketing gimmick when they introduced their new bread under the name "Kew-Bee," a phonetic spelling of the letters "QB."

To deliver their new products, the Stroehmanns purchased a new fleet of delivery vehicles, including seven wagons and three new trucks. Another promotional innovation was to have a three-day open house at the bakery to display the facility in operation. Few people had ever seen the inside of a bakery before and this did a great deal to publicize the operation. In less than a year, Stroehmann's output increased from 5,000 loaves to 25,000.

The Stroehmann brothers thought of their employees as an extended family. This was reflected in an annual tradition started in the 1930s and continuing into the 1970s of holding a full course Christmas dinner with gifts and entertainment for the employees, as an expression of appreciation for loyal service to the company. The Christmas party was held simultaneously in all seven of the Stroehmann's plants in Pennsylvania and New York. Their flagship bakery would be at 339 Washington Boulevard in Williamsport.

Both Harold and Carl were heavily involved in the Masonic and civic affairs of their adopted hometown. Harold J. Stroehmann Sr. died on January 24, 1954.

Carl retired from the day-to-day affairs of the company in 1955, moved to Florida, and turned over the reigns of the company to his nephew Harold J. "Frosty" Stroehmann Jr. Carl died at the age of 92 on February 16, 1989.

Frosty Stroehmann continued his family's hands-on and benevolent management of the bakery for almost 25 years. Like his father and uncle, Frosty was very active in Masonic and civic affairs, perhaps even more so. His best-known activity was his long and enthusiastic involvement with the Susquehanna Council of the Boy Scouts of America. He died at the age of 47 on July 29, 1978.

A little more than a year after Frosty's death, the Stroehmann's Bakery was sold to a Canadian firm, thus ending 55 years of local control of a business so widely identified with the Williamsport area. The only continuing presence of the Stroehmann Brothers' business in the area is a plant along Lycoming Creek Road in Old Lycoming Township that continues to operate.

THE ROBIN HOOD BOOTLEGGER

"Prince" David Farrington was born in Greensboro, North Carolina in 1890. At the age of 12, he was convicted of burning a barn owned by a neighbor who supposedly had tipped off the law about a still operated by Farrington's father. His first liquor law violation came in 1914 when he was fined $50 for selling whiskey without a license.

Farrington moved to Pennsylvania in 1920 and set about defying the Volstead Act, which established Prohibition. His Florida Fruit Farm was renowned for its hooch. When the long arm of the law could catch him, he did not resist. During one arrest, one of the revenue officers inventorying booze called out a certain number of barrels at 50-gallon capacity. Farrington then softly drawled, "I never saw those barrels in my life, but I'll bet you $100 that they don't have no more than forty gallons in them."

A generous man, he donated to churches and needy families, earning the nickname "Robin Hood of the farmers." A state liquor board investigator once remarked, "Farrington is truly a power in the community. The common fellow can always get a loan of from $5 on up. As a result, Farrington enjoys the friendship of all."

He paid farmers double the market value to forego raising wheat and oats to grow rye. A chemist who analyzed his liquor said it was superior to the average moonshine and a state liquor store manager said not only was it better than the state's product, but it was less expensive, too.

The *Gazette and Bulletin* newspaper reported once, "The local office of the State Liquor Control Board is to be commended on its action. It has never been charged that Farrington in any of his operations produced inferior liquor, but the fact that he has persisted in seeking to evade laws has made him a menace to society. The question asked frequently as to why, if he likes to manufacture liquor and seemingly has the ability to make a high quality, he does not go into the business in a legitimate way?"

Prince Farrington, the "Robin Hood Bootlegger," often fed and clothed needy families from the proceeds of his home-brewed "hooch." (WSG/GRIT.)

He often located his stills near underground springs and farms with only one entrance road, bragging that, "There is no power in the state of Pennsylvania sufficient to do me harm." The federal government reportedly spent more than $100,000 in prosecuting him throughout his "career." He died on June 14, 1956 at the age of 66.

Soldier and Statesman

Another entertaining individual who excelled in making friends and keeping their secrets was Henry W. Shoemaker. A man of versatility whose achievements crossed many differing fields, he was born to a wealthy family in New York City on February 24, 1882 and educated by private tutors at the Dr. E.D. Lyon's School in New York. Shoemaker graduated from Columbia University in 1900. During his childhood, he became interested in Pennsylvania's folklore while at his grandmother's farm near McElhattan. He would carry this interest for the rest of his life.

In 1904, Shoemaker entered the U.S. Foreign Service as a secretary to the delegation in Lisbon, Portugal, and later in the same capacity in Berlin. He returned to America in 1905 and was a member of the banking house of Shoemaker, Bates and Company until 1911. During this period, he began his military service as a member of the New York National Guard. When he moved to Pennsylvania, he became a member of the Pennsylvania National Guard. By the start of America's involvement in World War I in 1917, he was a lieutenant colonel on the staff of Governor Martin G. Brumbaugh.

Shoemaker bought two newspapers in Altoona in 1912, the *Tribune* and the *Gazette*, and later the *Altoona Times*. He combined these papers into the *Altoona Times-Tribune*. Under his stewardship, the *Times-Tribune* became one of Pennsylvania's most influential newspapers. He also published papers in Reading, Jersey Shore, and Bradford in Pennsylvania, and in Bridgeport, Connecticut.

After working as an intelligence officer in World War I, he returned to his newspaper activities and became very involved in Pennsylvania Republican

Waiting patiently is First Lieutenant Edward Smead, as soldier Anthony T. Cimini kisses his sister, Mary Cimini Usmar, good-bye. The train is loaded with soldiers waiting to depart for National Guard camp. Looking on is Cimini's mother, Mabel Cimini, and another sister, Rachael Cimini Smith. (WSG/GRIT.)

politics. He became close friends with several governors, a relationship that yielded him noteworthy appointments at the state level.

President Herbert Hoover summoned him back into the Foreign Service in 1930 as minister to Bulgaria where he served with distinction. He enjoyed the confidence of the highest councils of government in that country, including King Boris, who conferred Bulgaria's Order of Civil Merit in recognition of Shoemaker's services.

He returned to Pennsylvania in 1933 and continued his interest in the state's folklore and beauty, publishing numerous articles. Shoemaker was returned to military active duty in 1941 and served in the intelligence service. He was given a special citation by the War Department in 1943 for his service.

Following the war, he retired to his home, "Restless Oaks" at McElhattan in Clinton County. The tempo of his writing efforts quickened as he wrote several biographical works on historical figures such as Chief John Logan, Gifford Pinchot, and abolitionist John Brown. He remained active as a Mason, a member of the American Legion, Sons of the Revolution, and Sons of Union Veterans. Shoemaker died in Williamsport on July 15, 1958 at the age of 76.

RADIO DAYS WITH EV RUBENDALL

Ev Rubendall had a soft, reassuring voice that kept radio listeners in this area entertained and informed. Born in Williamsport on December 6, 1916, a son of John and Nora Shadle Rubendall, he later attended Williamsport High School and was introduced to the career that would mark his life. Rubendall was a sophomore and newspaper delivery boy in his neighborhood when he was asked to assume the role of a young lad in a radio mystery-drama, "Captain Darby and Jack." He assume his fictional guise three times a week for fifteen minutes. Once bitten with the bug for radio, Rubendall was hooked.

He started working for WRAK, Williamsport's first radio station, in 1939. Among his duties were to assist Sol "Woody" Wolf with broadcasts of Williamsport Grays games. They covered the away games from the studios of WRAK, receiving information on the action from a teletype ticker. He and Wolf used inventive sound effects to make the audience believe that the two were actually at the ball game.

He also did other announcing stints for the station in the afternoons and evenings until he enlisted in the armed services in 1942. He rejoined the WRAK announcing staff after he returned in 1946, becoming the morning announcer, a time slot he held for the next 33 years.

"Rube" developed warmth and a rapport with his listeners, having a genuine interest in them that they had no trouble sensing. His voice was noted as one of calmness and warmth—the type of soothing voice that was needed when he would have to report bad news such as assassinations, wars, or other tragedies. When floods struck the Susquehanna Valley in 1946 and 1972, his professionalism and sensitivity were instrumental in helping many get through those trying times.

An American Red Cross volunteer gives magazines and other reading material to GIs departing during World War II from the railroad station at the Park Hotel. (WSG/GRIT.)

Marian, his wife of 50 years, remembered him as "a kind and gentle family man. He treated his listeners like they were a member of the family. He was a wonderful man and everyone whoever knew him felt that way." Rubendall retired from WRAK in 1980, but he continued to give of himself to others. His intense interest in local history led to him becoming the research manager for the Lycoming County Historical Museum.

A MODERN-DAY PAUL REVERE

One Williamsport man, Joseph L. Lockard, will forever be entwined with the tragic story of the Japanese attack on Pearl Harbor on December 7, 1941.

Lockard was born in Williamsport on October 30, 1922, a son of George and Dorothy Lockard of 918 Race Street. According to Lockard's sister Ethel, her father was only bringing home $7 per week from his job as a mechanic at Richardson Buick to support five people at the depth of the Great Depression.

Lockard dropped out of high school and enlisted in the army in August 1940 with two of his friends, John Albright and Donald Cook. After basic training, Lockard went to Fort Slocomb, near New Rochelle, New York, where he was assigned to work on mines to protect New York Harbor. He was transferred

Joseph Lockard was a Williamsport radar operator during World War II. He notified army authorities that Japanese planes were approaching Pearl Harbor on December 7, 1941, but his warnings were ignored. He was treated as a hero and rose from the rank of private to that of second lieutenant. (LCHS.)

by army transport ship to duty in the Philippines, but Lockard and Albright disembarked in Hawaii because the army was recruiting members for a new unit, the Signal Company Aircraft Warning.

In November 1941, Lockard was detailed to a mobile radar unit at Opana on the northern tip of Oahu. He was working on the morning of December 7, and the shift ended at 7 a.m., but Lockard did not shut down his radar equipment. He recounted the following:

> Shortly after 7 we started getting one large blip. When I saw the large blip I thought maybe something was wrong with our equipment. We had no idea what the blip was showing. It was moving too fast to be any ships so it had to be something in the air. We tried to plot its course. We were able to determine at the moment we saw the blip, that turned out to be the attacking planes, was probably about 137 miles out. I think the Jap carriers were about 200 miles out.

He called Fort Shafter:

> There was no one at the plotting center except a switchboard operator. He said everyone there was out to breakfast. We finally got a hold of a

> Lieutenant Kermit Tyler about 7:20 a.m. Tyler assured us that the blip we saw was an inbound flight of B-17s that was due in that morning. The planes were coming in from the north though. If they were that far off course they never would have made the islands.

Lockard continued to plot the planes and lost them about 20 miles out because of interference. He said they closed up the radar unit about 8 a.m. when the truck came and picked them up. On the way to breakfast, a truck sped their way with soldiers frantically waving and yelling at them to get their attention, then they noticed black billows of smoke and realized something catastrophic had happened.

The world found out about Lockard's alertness in February 1942 when a congressman on the Roberts Commission investigating the Pearl Harbor debacle released the information. The news accounts of the time compared Lockard to a "modern-day Paul Revere." He was sent back to Washington to receive the Distinguished Service Medal and his family witnessed the ceremony.

Lockard and his family met Vice President Henry Wallace, Assistant Secretary of War Robert Patterson, and numerous congressman. He then was sent to

These happy youths are perched atop a car in downtown Williamsport after hearing the news that Japan has surrendered on August 14, 1945. (LCHS.)

Officer Candidate School, and after being promoted and sent to advanced radio school, Lockard was assigned to the Aleutian Islands, where he was stationed for more than a year. He left the service in December 1945, eventually retiring in Harrisburg with his wife, the former Pauline Seidel.

CAPTURING HISTORY ON FILM

For more than 55 years, Putsee Vannucci has captured the tears, the joys, the great, the near-great, the humble personages, the great events, and the small events of the greater Williamsport area and beyond through the lens of a camera. These enduring photographic images serve as a scrapbook of life in the area during these years.

Vannucci, son of John and Josephine Girardi Vannucci, was born on March 17, 1921. The photography bug bit him fairly early while at Curtin Junior High School. Putsee would pick up various photographic supplies for the school's camera club at Hoyer's, which was then located on Market Street. In high school, Vannucci used his budding photographic talent to take photos for the school yearbook, *La Memoire*.

After graduating from high school, his older brother invited him to join him in California where he was a steward at several racetrack restaurants. His brother suggested that it would be a good place to get a college education since California's junior colleges were publicly funded and students paid little tuition. Putsee was paid to take photographs of the winning horses and their jockeys at the various racetracks, and his future on the West Coast appeared bright until his mother's health deteriorated and someone was needed to look after her. His brother was just about to enlist in the navy, so Putsee was designated to return to Williamsport.

He briefly worked in a local furniture factory before taking a photography job in the advertising department of the *Sun-Gazette*. Then came what may have been his big break. A large dam near Austin in Potter County broke, causing great destruction in that area, and the Red Cross needed photographs to document the destruction. He borrowed the *Williamsport Sun*'s solitary camera, which was shared in those days by that paper and the *Gazette and Bulletin*. Vannucci brought the film back and had it processed, and sports editor Lou Pickelner suggested that he write a story about what he saw in Austin. After that, the editorial department asked that Vannucci be transferred, and his first "beat" became city hall, the courthouse, police and fire, and the hospitals.

Vannucci worked for a couple of other newspapers in the region before returning to Williamsport and joining the *Gazette and Bulletin* staff, where he remained until shortly after the war ended. When the servicemen came home, they were guaranteed their old jobs and Vannucci was released to make room for a returning veteran. He was classified as "4-F" and couldn't serve in the armed forces.

In 1946, he and his brother Art opened their own commercial photography business, which received an unintended boost in May 1946 when a flood devastated the Williamsport area. They took many photos of the damage and created a commemorative photo album that sold successfully. The profits helped to expand and consolidate the Vannuccis' fledgling business.

Starting in 1947, Vannucci would begin one of his most enduring and noteworthy assignments: the annual Little League Baseball World Series. Vannucci is the only photographer to have shot every series and was honored by Little League when he threw out the first pitch at the 50th championship game in 1996.

The World Series produced Vannucci's favorite moment as a photographer when, in 1976, Joe DiMaggio was a guest of Little League. "DiMaggio was great. He mixed with all the kids and went to both dugouts. He was a real gentleman and it was a thrill to photograph him," Vannucci recalled. He said DiMaggio's conduct was a contrast to Mickey Mantle's behavior several years earlier. "Mantle didn't want anything to do with the kids and he wouldn't sign any autographs."

Much of the photographic work that Vannucci did was as contract work for both the *Grit* and the *Sun-Gazette*. He covered all the major fires, floods, plane crashes, and accidents, as well as visits by celebrities to the area. Many of Vannucci's celebrity photos can be seen on the walls of the Genetti Hotel and Convention Center. He also worked as a public relations photographer for Susquehanna University for 30 years.

Illegal slot machines are smashed in a crackdown during the 1940s by members of the Lycoming County District Attorney's Office and area police officials. (WSG/GRIT.)

Vannucci was a founder and charter member of the North Central Pennsylvania Photographers Association. In 1999, he was inducted into the West Branch Valley Chapter of the Pennsylvania Sports Hall of Fame. He still takes photographs on occasion. However, he has not chosen to embrace digital cameras, although he has his own computer and is an avid Internet user. Thousands of negatives of Vannucci's work are preserved in the annals of the Lycoming County Historical Museum so the breadth of local history that he has witnessed can be enjoyed by future generations.

THE MUSICAL MAYOR

One of the most colorful politicians ever to hold office in the area was Leo C. Williamson, mayor of Williamsport for a record 12 years.

Born in 1899, Williamson worked at various jobs as a young man, including driving a bread truck. In the 1920s, he worked his way up to sales manager for a local bakery, and in 1932, he opened a combination restaurant, bakery,

Firemen spray water onto a fire at the Lycoming County Historical Society and Museum in 1960. The museum was the former mansion of Judge John W. Maynard, and it was replaced in the late 1960s. (LCHS.)

The colorful Leo Williamson, mayor of Williamsport, purchases war bonds at Stearns Department Store during World War II. Williamson served as Williamsport's mayor from 1940 to 1952. (LCHS.)

and delicatessen on West Fourth Street. It was a popular gathering spot for the downtown crowd where Williamson gained the reputation as a jovial, easy-going raconteur who enjoyed people of all types and classes.

He loved to sing and first performed publicly as a member of the Newberry Methodist Church choir. In 1918, he and three high school friends formed the Keystone Male Quartet, which sang for conventions and banquets for 30 years.

Williamson's popularity with people of all walks of life prompted Republican Party leaders to ask him to run for mayor in 1939. He won the first of three terms that year, but he is best remembered not for some great building project, but the "Community and Kiddies Sings" he initiated at the Brandon Park band shell. In his first year in office, he started the Community Sing as a way to highlight Williamsport's musical talent and to bring free, wholesome entertainment to its residents. The following year, he started a Kiddies Sing that helped encourage a younger generation of singers and musicians, one of his proudest accomplishments because they wedded two of Williamson's main passions, music and civic pride. The "sings" were a popular fixture into the 1960s.

While mayor, Williamson helped to create the Williamsport Water Authority and the Williamsport Airport Authority. He led the city through the difficult years of World War II and helped to get its citizens behind the nation's war effort,

Vice President Richard Nixon, right, visited Williamsport rallying support for his political ambitions. A beaming Mayor Leo Williamson, center, basks in the presence of the man who became the only president to resign his office. At left is Quinton E. Beauge, a former general manager and executive editor of the Williamsport Sun-Gazette. *Beauge served as president of the Pennsylvania Newspaper Publishers Association and as president of the Pennsylvania Associated Press. (WSG/GRIT.)*

using his promotional talent to lead paper, rubber, and scrap drives, as well as War Bond drives.

He loved sports and once said, "Competitive sports, played under the rules, is the greatest thing a country can know. It's the greatest character builder I know." It was one of his greatest pleasures as mayor to preside over the opening of the Williamsport Grays baseball during his time in office, and he was one of Little League's earliest and most ardent boosters.

In one of the greatest upsets in Williamsport's political history, city voters rejected his bid for a fourth term in November 1951, electing former policeman Clifford Harman. Williamson died at the age of 58 on August 13, 1957.

A REDISCOVERED WRITER

Like many artists, the works of H. Beam Piper lacked appreciation, especially monetarily, while he lived. But since his death, Piper's science fiction writings have attained a cult-like following and belated appreciation from aficionados of the genre.

Piper was born in Altoona in 1904. Little is known of his early years, as he was always guarded about his personal life. He was largely self-educated, with a deep interest in history and science, saying he obtained his knowledge "without subjecting myself to the ridiculous misery of four years in the uncomfortable confines of a raccoon coat" to illustrate his discomfort with institutions of higher learning.

At the age of 18, he worked as a laborer and later as a guard for the Pennsylvania Railroad. His earliest published work was "Flight From Tomorrow," which appeared in the September/October 1950 issue of *Future* magazine. Throughout the 1950s and early 1960s, Piper published several stories in science fiction and fantasy magazines, as well as a number of science fiction novels. Among the most notable: *A Planet for Texans*, 1958; *Four Day Planet*, 1961; *Space Viking*, 1962; *Little Fuzzy*, 1962; and *Junkyard Planet*, 1963.

Railroad men from the New York Central and Pennsylvania Railroad shake hands fraternally after the merger of their rail lines was announced in 1966. The Penn Central Railroad would eventually go bankrupt. (LCHS.)

Piper moved to Williamsport in 1957, living for seven years at 330 East Third Street, using Williamsport and Lycoming County as the setting for several tales. Piper expressed his view of science fiction this way:

> Science fiction has come up from the wrong side of the tracks. In years past it was associated with pulp magazines, with lurid covers. In recent years, however, the top slick magazines and book publishers have been featuring it. It is potentially a fine form of literature if the author knows what he wants to say and how to say it. But it is getting harder and harder for science fiction writers to stay ahead of science.

Despite having his work appearing throughout the world and carving his own niche in the science-fiction community, he had little money to show for it. He summarized, "My world seems to have shrunk to the size of my desktop in one dimension, while expanding out through the galaxy in another." By early November 1964, he was down to $1.59, his latest manuscript rejected by a publisher. He was reduced to eating pigeons that he shot with a gun from his formerly extensive collection of antique firearms. On November 9, 1964, Piper shut off all the utilities to his apartment, put painter's drop cloths over the walls and floors, and shot himself.

His suicide note may reveal what Piper was like. It read in part, "I don't like to leave messes when I go away, but if I could have cleaned up any of this mess, I wouldn't be going away."

Many of Piper's surviving manuscripts were stored and later published, particularly by Ace Books, and several World Wide Web pages are devoted to his work, garnering recognition in death that he never attained in life. Jerry Pournelle, in his preface to *Federation*, a collection of some of Piper's works, provides what might be a fitting epitaph:

> He knew the grand sweep of history, but he knew the small tales; the intrigues and petty jealousies, heroism and cowardice, honor and betrayals. This is why his stories have such a ring of truth. . . . He was a storyteller, a man who could keep you up all night with his books and tales. He was a cavalier.

12. On the Shoulders of Giants

The flash flood on Antes Creek in June 1889 claimed the lives of nine people in John C. Youngman's family. Determined that no Williamsport family would have to suffer this devastating tragedy again, he spearheaded an effort to create a dike system to protect the city.

Youngman was born on January 25, 1903 in Williamsport. One of his forebears was Colonel John Henry Antes who erected the stockade fort in 1776 that became known as Antes Fort. The Youngman family owned large plots of land in what is now the Newberry section of Williamsport, particularly in the area around West Hills Estate. Another part of the Youngman family founded Mifflinburg in nearby Union County.

Youngman graduated from the Wharton School of Business in 1924 and Harvard Law School in 1927. After opening a law practice locally, he successfully ran for Lycoming County district attorney, serving from 1932 to 1936. During his tenure, he did not seek the death penalty for criminals because he did not believe in capital punishment "because you can't correct a mistake if you make it."

He initiated a flood-control campaign in 1935, traveling to Washington, D.C. to seek federal aid for the project. Franklin Roosevelt's "New Deal" had funded thousands of public works projects across the country as a means of fighting unemployment, and Youngman believed a dike project for Williamsport would qualify. If the dike project had been completed in the mid-1930s, the cost would have been about $125,000. When the project was finally completed in 1952, the cost was about $6 million.

Ironically, the major roadblock to the dike project was not in Washington but locally. City council and various other local business leaders were against the project, believing the dikes would wash out frequently. The people of Williamsport were ravaged again by flooding in March 1936, and after much lobbying and cajoling, Youngman persuaded city council to put the dike issue to the voters. In November 1940, the city's voters decided the matter. Ironically, and perhaps providentially, heavy rains lashed the Williamsport area on election day, filling area streams and the Susquehanna River almost to their banks. Voters soundly approved a dike system by a large margin.

This unfortunate bull was washed into the tree by the swift and unrelenting waters during the flood of June 1, 1889, one of the most devastating floods in Williamsport. (LCHS.)

The work on the dikes was scheduled to begin in late 1941, but America's entry in World War II interrupted construction. Williamsporters were reminded again of the need for the dike system in May 1946 when high waters once again wreaked havoc. Work had restarted on the dikes, but they were not in place at the time of the flood. It would be six more years before they would be finished.

Other area infrastructure issues concerned Youngman as well. He served on the Williamsport Sanitary Authority and was chairman of the Williamsport Municipal Water Authority, and he was a driving force in having fluoride placed in the city's water supply.

The environment concerned Youngman, too, and during his time on the Susquehanna River Basin Commission, he pushed for the clean up of mine acid and raw sewage from the waterway. Fishing and the outdoors were an abiding passion for him—he especially loved fly-fishing on Antes Creek.

Even at 88 years of age, he continued to come to work every day at his law office. He had an active interest in Williamsport's fraternal and social club scene. He was a Mason, a member of the Ross Club, and active with the Boys Club of America and local Masonic and civic organizations. When he died at the age of 97, Youngman left an enduring legacy of a safer, cleaner, and healthier Williamsport.

MAX MILLER'S CHILD OF HOPE

No one did more to improve the lives of the mentally disabled of this area, particularly children, than Dr. Max C. Miller. He accomplished this through the founding of the School of Hope, later known as Hope Enterprises.

He was born in Montgomery on December 15, 1911, the son of John Ray Miller and Elizabeth "Mabel" Miller. He attended Montgomery schools and graduated from Penn State University, then received his medical degree from Temple University Medical School. He met a student nurse, Leona, while on his residency at Williamsport Hospital, and they married in June 1939.

Miller initially was a general practitioner, but his love for children motivated him to specialize in pediatrics, studying at the Elizabethtown State Hospital for Crippled Children and the Pittsburgh Children's Hospital.

The Millers' daughter, Mary Lynn, was born in 1943, and her father soon noticed that she had problems sitting up and seemed slow developmentally. He suspected

Overturned vehicles are part of the damage wrought in the aftermath of the 1936 flood. A 1940 vote approved dikes to control the rainwater. (LCHS.)

she was mentally retarded, but chose not to reveal his fears to his wife right away. Mary Lynn served as a catalyst for Miller's choice to work with the disabled.

In the 1940s and 1950s, parents often chose to institutionalize retarded children because there were no agencies to provide support. Leona later recalled, "It seemed as though you were encouraged to hide or shut away the children from society and Max and I knew we could never do that to Mary Lynn."

The Millers and other families of the area began a support network to help each other deal with the challenges they encountered. It was from this network that the idea emerged of a school for the children—the School of Hope. By the 1950s, the families decided that a handicapped-accessible school should be built. They launched fundraisers and asked for donations from various area businesses, service clubs, and philanthropists to aid the effort. On September 30, 1958, the new School of Hope was opened at 1536 Catherine Street. Governor George Leader visited and was so impressed he said the school could be a pattern for counties throughout the Commonwealth.

Miller and his wife received the *Grit*'s Community Service Award in 1960, and the school received the Benjamin Rush Award from the Pennsylvania

John C. Youngman with shovel, along with other Williamsport and area officials, is about to break ground in 1940 for the flood control dike system that will eventually help to protect Williamsport and its environs against the ravages of flooding. (WSG/GRIT.)

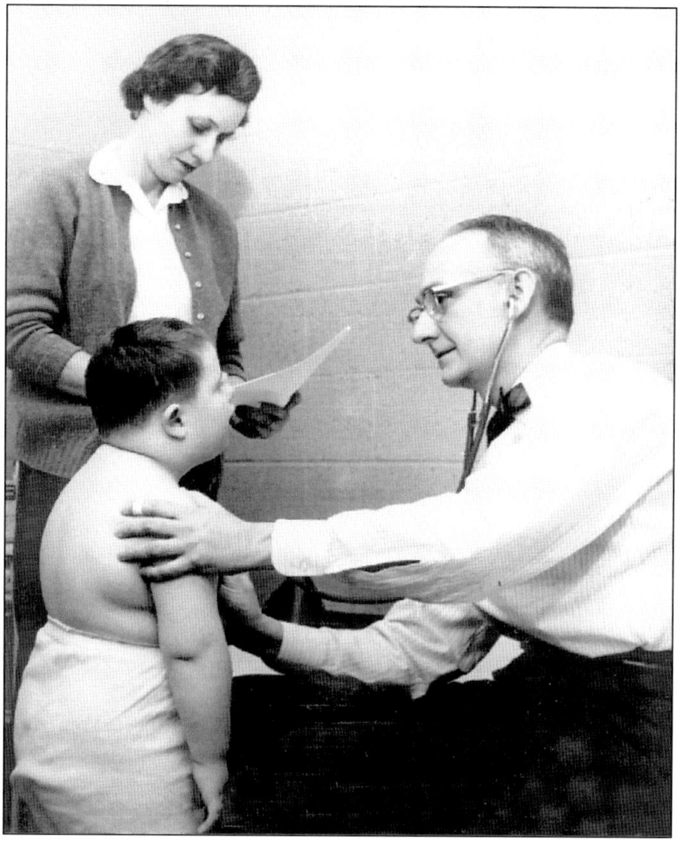

Dr. Max Miller, founder of the School of Hope (later Hope Enterprises), a social service that has served mentally disabled clients for more than 50 years, examines one of his young patients. (WSG/GRIT.)

Medical Society in 1961. Miller helped oversee the growth of the School of Hope throughout the rest of his life, and set a foundation for its expansion into Hope Enterprises in the 1970s.

Miller died on November 1, 1971, leaving behind a living monument that continues to serve the needs of the mentally challenged into the future.

He Invented the Zip Code

The man who invented the zip code, Robert Aurand Moon, was born and raised in Williamsport. His death warranted a four-column, above-the-fold obituary in the *New York Times*, as well as notations in such large metropolitan newspapers as the *Los Angeles Times*, the *Washington Post*, and the *Miami Herald*, and was noted by Peter Jennings on *ABC News*.

Moon was born April 15, 1917, a son of John and Eva Moon. He graduated from Williamsport High School, where he met his high school sweetheart, Barbara Packard, whom he eventually married on April 12, 1939. In 1940, he worked as a postal carrier and a clerk, and in 1942, he took the inspector's exam. While an inspector, he received training in criminal investigation and performed so efficiently that post office officials in Washington intervened to prevent his enlistment in the army during World War II.

During the war, he was assigned to several post offices in the Philadelphia Region and engaged in some secret investigations that helped uncover espionage activities using post office channels. It was while working in the Philadelphia Region in 1944 that Moon developed the idea that would become the zip code. Moon presciently was able to see that trains would eventually be supplanted by air transportation to move people, goods, and mail, and thought developing something like the zip code would help to expedite the delivery of mail.

By 1962, Postmaster General Lawrence Day and other postal authorities could see the merits of Moon's proposed Zoning Improvement Plan, or "Zip," and approved the idea. The zip code program was officially adopted by the post office on July 1, 1963 and mail delivery has never been the same since. Moon's zip code innovation quite possibly has saved billions of dollars. Interestingly, the postal service will not give Moon full credit for inventing the zip code. A spokesman for the United States Postal Service said, "proper credit goes to a committee." He died in Leesburg, Florida on April 10, 2001.

THE KEYSTONE SHORTWAY

Few highways have so thoroughly affected the economic life of the northcentral Pennsylvania region more than the Keystone Shortway, now better known as Interstate 80. The moving force behind the building of the road was Zehnder H. "Dick" Confair, born in Berwick on January 11, 1906, son of Charles F. and Rena Baum Confair.

After attending the public schools of Berwick, he went to the prestigious Wharton School of Business at the University of Pennsylvania. He opened a soft-drink bottling company in 1933, operating the Confair Bottling Company for almost 50 years. His involvement in business prompted a long-term interest in economic and industrial development for the area, and he was the first chairman of the Greater Williamsport Chamber of Commerce Industrial Development Bureau.

In the mid-1950s, Confair became interested in the concept of a "Keystone Shortway," a four-lane interstate highway that would link the markets and people of northcentral Pennsylvania with larger markets in New York, Philadelphia, and Pittsburgh. His interest in a Keystone Shortway coincided with President Dwight Eisenhower's drive to create a modern interstate highway system. Confair was in a better position to further his dream for the Shortway when he was elected to the state senate in 1958, where he served for 14 years until poor health caused him to retire from public life.

Confair's dream was realized on September 17, 1970, when the 313-mile Keystone Shortway was opened. The Shortway, and a bridge crossing the Susquehanna River near Milton, bears his name. In 1970, Confair received the *Grit*'s Community Service Award. He died on January 26, 1982.

Philanthropic "Bill" Pickelner

Perhaps nobody has played a more integral part in bettering the Greater Williamsport area in a variety of community-service arenas in the past 50 years than William "Bill" Pickelner. He is a member of numerous boards of directors, has received dozens of well-deserved honors, and few in the community have not at least heard his name.

Born of Russian Jewish immigrants Phillip and Anna Pickelner in Williamsport on September 14, 1914, his is the quintessential American success story. His father worked as a peddler with a horse and wagon. It is from his father that Pickelner believes he developed his sense of service to others. "My dad was a very philanthropic man. He never turned anyone away who needed help. He loved people. I think that caring for others rubbed off on me," Pickelner said.

Even before graduating from high school Pickelner became involved in the business that would develop into his livelihood—coal and fuel sales. In 1932, he

Bill "Buck" Byham, affectionately known as "The Lefthander," has announced local sports on the radio for decades. He still announces at the annual Little League Baseball World Series and is a sports writer for both the Internet and the print media. (SG/GRIT.)

would often travel to the Wilkes-Barre area and other places in the coal region with a truck to buy fuel for his fledgling business. His father helped him in the office, handling many of the administrative chores. Pickelner's first taste of community service came when he became involved with the Jewish philanthropic organization B'nai B'rith, about 1935. On March 21, 1935, he married a woman named Sara.

About that same time, Pickelner became deeply involved with an activity he always loved and in which he remains active today—professional baseball. A former batboy for the 1923 Williamsport Grays, he became a member of the board of the directors of the Williamsport Grays in the mid-1930s. He led B'nai B'rith to become involved in the promotional activities of the ballclub at Bowman Field. In 1955, the sponsoring of a special event by the group allowed the Williamsport Grays to finish the season, after the team ran into financial difficulty.

Bowman Field has always been a second home for Pickelner, so when the Bowman Field Commission was established by the city in 1957 to administer the uptown ballpark, it was only natural that Pickelner become a member. Today, he serves as its chairman.

Whenever the future of professional baseball in the city was in doubt, Pickelner always took the lead in trying to keep it viable. Most recently, in 1993, he was the catalyst in bringing the Geneva Cubs to Williamsport, and the owners of Geneva Baseball, Inc. have had one of the longest relationships with the city's baseball fans since the golden days of the Grays in the 1930s and 1940s.

Baseball isn't the only sport in which Pickelner took a keen interest. From 1947 to 1964, he owned and operated the Williamsport Billies basketball team of the professional Eastern Basketball League.

Pickelner's leadership and enthusiasm have assisted most capital campaigns benefiting charitable groups. He was two-time campaign chairman for the Lycoming United Way, and other organizations that benefited from his help are United Jewish Appeal, Lycoming College, Williamsport Hospital, the School of Hope, the Pennsylvania College of Technology, Salvation Army, Divine Providence Hospital, the Williamsport Home, and the YMCA, to name a few. He was the building force behind the new arena at the YWCA, which now bears his name because of the persuasive powers he used in helping to find the money in the community to see the arena built.

Floods Continue to Ravage Valley

Even with all the improved flood protection brought to the Williamsport area by the U.S. Army Corps of Engineers in the late 1940s and early 1950s, the flooding of area waterways continue to be an endemic problem for the area. The rains dumped on the area from the remnants of Hurricane Agnes in June 1972 caused millions of dollars in damage. Fortunately, because of flood protection improvements, Williamsport was spared from the worst of it, although barely so, as the Susquehanna came perilously close to overflowing the dike system. Outlying areas were not so fortunate. The watersheds of Lycoming, Loyalsock,

Pennsylvania Governor Tom Ridge comforts a resident at a shelter in Old Lycoming Township Fire Company in the aftermath of the 1996 flood, which devastated the region after warm temperatures, melting snow, and rain flooded area creeks. Ridge would later serve as the nation's first director of Homeland Security. (WSG/GRIT.)

and Pine Creeks were badly damaged, and thousands were displaced for months. Three years later, in September, the remnants of another storm, Eloise, caused extensive damage to the area, but not on the scale of 1972.

The most deadly of recent floods occurred on January 19, 1996. Melting snow and soaking rains caused by unseasonably warm temperatures caused area streams to go on the rampage, particularly the Lycoming Creek watershed. That flood claimed the lives of six people. Several victims were drowned in their trailers at trailer parks located in Lycoming, Old Lycoming, and Lewis Townships. In addition to the lives lost, the flood caused millions of dollars in damage, dislocating many families and causing the demise of several businesses.

THE TRAGEDY OF TWA FLIGHT 800

Tragedy for the area continued in 1996, when 16 French club students from Montoursville High School, along with their 5 adult chaperones, perished in the crash of TWA Flight 800 off Long Island on July 17, 1996.

This tragedy plunged the Susquehanna Valley into deep mourning and placed the area in the intense, unwanted glare of national and international publicity

Volunteers scramble to pile sandbags against the dike in South Williamsport as protection against the rising West Branch of the Susquehanna during the 1972 flood produced by the remnants of Hurricane Agnes. (WSG/GRIT.)

as victims' families were pursued for interviews. Reporters and camera crews flooded into Montoursville, some of them seemingly unfeeling and uncaring regarding the families' desire for private grieving.

The crash was shrouded in controversy as conspiracy theorists offered up their own causes, ranging from a terrorist attack to "friendly fire" as a result of an errant missile fired by the U.S. Navy. Several years later, the National Transportation Safety Board finally ruled that the cause was mechanical.

LITTLE LEAGUE HELPS KEEP WILLIAMSPORT IN SPOTLIGHT

Little League Baseball, with more than 2.7 million players in 105 countries, continues to put Williamsport and Lycoming County on the map, as it has for several decades. Providing stewardship for Little League through the 1970s and 1980s was Dr. Creighton J. Hale, a pioneer in sports safety who patented the radial-ribbed batting helmet design still in use today worldwide. A new generation of Little League leaders takes the program into the new century, with Stephen

D. Keener at the helm. Keener is the first Little League graduate to become the organization's president and CEO.

Visitors come from around the world to watch the Little League Baseball World Series every August, and the tournament itself expanded from eight teams to sixteen in 2001. A second stadium, Little League Volunteer Stadium, was built to accommodate the extra games, joining venerable old Howard J. Lamade Stadium on the 66-acre Little League Baseball International Complex.

An angel memorializes the 21 Montoursville Area High School French Club students and their chaperones who perished on TWA Flight 800 in 1996. (WSG/GRIT.)

Little League itself has weathered several controversies over the years. Girls were finally admitted to the program in 1974, but only after Little League was sued in 20 states. Taiwan dominated the Series for nearly three decades and charges of stacking teams were rampant—although Little League never disqualified any Taiwanese teams from the Series for irregularities. That dubious honor fell to Zamboanga City Little League, Philippines, in 1992, for using players from outside the local league's boundaries. In 2001, the Rolando Paulino Little League team from the Bronx, New York, was stripped of its third-place finish when it was discovered belatedly that flame-throwing pitcher Danny Almonte was 14 years old—two years too old for Little League.

It was not, however, enough to detract from the pageantry of the first visit by a sitting U.S. president to a Little League World Series. George W. Bush (the first Little Leaguer to become president) arrived in Williamsport via Air Force One

Dr. Creighton Hale, former president and CEO of Little League Baseball, Incorporated, and innovator in safety equipment for youth sports, is faced with a crisis in 1973. A lawsuit (one of many) was filed on behalf of New Jersey's Maria Pepe by the National Organization for Women, eventually forcing Little League to include girls in its all-boys baseball program in 1974. (LLB.)

President George W. Bush, a former Little Leaguer, delivers a speech at the 2001 Little League Baseball World Series. He also delivered the ceremonial first pitch and is the only sitting President to have attended a Little League World Series game. (LLB.)

and, after a short motorcade to South Williamsport, delivered the ceremonial first pitch before the final game. He then watched from the stands for three innings as teams from Tokyo, Japan, and Apopka, Florida, squared off amid extraordinary security at Lamade Stadium.

President Bush and First Lady Laura Bush, ardent baseball fans and Little League supporters, annually host Tee Ball on the South Lawn games at the White House, in which Little League teams are invited to play "in the people's back yard." Little League officials from the Williamsport area make several trips to the White House each year to plan and administer the games for President Bush.

Security was tight again at the 2002 Little League World Series, but not because of a presidential visit. Little League officials, along with local, state, and federal authorities, boosted security at the international event as a result of the September 11, 2001 terror attacks. But, as always, admission remained free for the Series, which annually draws more than 40,000 people to the final game.

REVIVING DOWNTOWN WILLIAMSPORT

Like many cities, with the advent of malls and superstores, downtown businesses have suffered as they have been forced to change from primarily retail to service and support. Because of this, various strategies have been advanced to revitalize the downtown areas, the most ambitious being a proposed $72-million plan that would integrate a new Market Street Bridge with riverfront recreational facilities and possibly even a downtown civic arena. The proposal is still on the drawing board, so it remains to be seen if revitalization will work, and if additional jobs and commerce will result.

A few visionaries look to the arts to help revitalize the sluggish downtown and hope to make Williamsport one of the "best, small art towns" in the United States. Several organizations have shouldered the responsibility to improve Williamsport's public relations and encourage visitors downtown, including OurTowns: 2010, MainStreet, and the First Friday Arts Town committee. By collaborating with various arts organizations and local businesses, the group has introduced monthly cultural events and annual festivals.

Local civic leaders are looking to use Williamsport's hosting of two colleges (Lycoming College and Pennsylvania College of Technology), an educated workforce in the pursuit of technology industries, and the quality of life found in the Williamsport area as assets to be transformed to the creation of more jobs and tourism. It seems that Williamsport and Lycoming County are in

A resident outfitted in traditional attire sells African crafts at the Summerfest at Brandon Park in 1993. Celebrating their cultural heritage, Williamsport residents stage an annual festival that has taken several forms, from an Afro-American Fest to the more recent Juneteenth, held in Brandon Park. (WSG/GRIT.)

a transitional period that is open to the imagination and vision of those who live there.

One of the ways in which Williamsport seeks to revive itself is to take advantage of the region's cultural diversity. Underappreciated and overlooked for many years, this diversity has become a remedy for the economic planners and organizers in the form of festivals and celebrations.

One summertime event that draws visitors to Brandon Park is the annual Afro-American Fest that has evolved into the Juneteenth celebration. Juneteenth is considered the date when the last slaves in America were freed. Actual emancipation did not come until General Gordon Granger rode into Galveston, Texas and issued General Order No. 3, on June 19, 1865, almost two and a half years after President Abraham Lincoln signed the Emancipation Proclamation. Lincoln issued the proclamation on September 22, 1862, notifying the states in rebellion against the Union that if they did not cease their rebellion and return to the Union by January 1, 1863, he would declare their slaves forever free. The proclamation was ignored by those states that seceded from the Union and as a result, 800,000 slaves were unaffected. It would take a civil war to enforce the Emancipation Proclamation and the 13th Amendment to the U.S. Constitution to formally outlaw slavery in the United States.

Another revival of a cultural event is held on the river at the Susquehanna State Park, the Hiawatha Riverfest Regatta. The regatta was revived in the summer of 2003 after a 46-year hiatus and benefits the Hiawatha Paddlewheel Boat and various charities. The event draws about 150 entries with boats from 10 to 12 feet and includes runabouts and hydroplanes that can reach speeds of between 60 and 80 miles per hour. It is historically appropriate that the regatta—an event that draws thousands of visitors to the river—takes place on the Susquehanna near the site of the historic Susquehanna Boom because of the economic importance of the boom during Williamsport's and the surrounding area's heyday as the "Lumber Capital of the World."

BIBLIOGRAPHY

Anspach, Marshall R., ed. *Historical Sketches of the Bench and Bar of Lycoming County, Pennsylvania, 1795–1960*. Williamsport: Lycoming Law Association, 1961.

Bakeless, John Edwin. *Turncoats, Traitors and Heroes*. Philadelphia: J.B. Lippincott, 1959.

Boyd, Andrew and W.H. Boyd. *Directory of Williamsport*. Reading, PA: W.H. Boyd Company, 1866–1960.

Bray, George A. III. "The Delicate Art of Scalping." *Muzzleloader Magazine* 13.2 (1986): 54–56.

Byrne, Thomas. "Elmira's Civil War Prison Camp: 1864-65." *Chemung County Historical Journal* 9 (1964): 1298.

Chemung County Historical Journal, 1955–2003.

Clarke, W.P. *The Life and Times of the Honorable William Fisher Packer*. Williamsport: Lycoming County Historical Society, 1937.

Coryell, Tunnison. "Autobiographical Sketches of Tunnison Coryell, 1791–1881." Unpublished manuscript. Williamsport: James V. Brown Library.

Cummings, Michael. *Mike Cummings Remembers . . . Hobos, Ragmen, Mean Old Dogs and Francis of Assisi*. Williamsport: Grit Publishing, 1983.

Daily Gazette and Bulletin, 1872–1955.

Dornsife, Samuel and Eleanor M. Wolfson. *Lost Williamsport*. Williamsport: Riverrun Productions, 1995.

Fink, Carlton E. Sr. "Robert Covenhoven, 1876, A Biographical Sketch." *Journal of the Lycoming County Historical Society* 4 (1967): 6–8.

Freeze, John G. *Pennsylvania Magazine of History and Biography*, Vol. 3. Philadelphia: The Historical Society of Pennsylvania, 1879.

The Grit, 1882–1984.

Humes, James C. *Sweet Dreams: Tales of a River City*. Williamsport: Grit Publishing, 1966.

Jackson, Anna. Personal journal entry, August 1778, reprinted in *Now and Then* 16 (1971): 360.

Journal of the Lycoming County Historical Society, 1955–2003.

Kent, Barry C. *Susquehanna's Indians*. Harrisburg: Pennsylvania Historical and Museum Commission, 1984.

Lloyd, Thomas W. *History of Lycoming County*. 2 vols. Topeka, IN: Historical Publishing Company, 1929.

Lycoming Gazette, 1807–1836.

Mack, John Martin. Personal journal entry. Lycoming County Pennsylvania Genealogy Project, 1753.

Meginness, John F. *History of Lycoming County Including Its Aboriginal History*. Chicago: Brown, 1892.

———. *Otzinachson: A History of the West Branch Valley of the Susquehanna*. Philadelphia: John F. Meginness, 1857.

Pennsylvania Writers Projects of the W.P.A. *A Picture of Lycoming County*. Williamsport: Commissions of Lycoming County, 1939.

Philadelphia Evening Bulletin, 1847–1982.

Pomeroy, A. *Atlas of Lycoming County*. Philadelphia: A. Pomeroy & Co., 1873.

Rhian, Terry. "Williamsport's Economic Development During the Canal Period, 1820-1850." Unpublished paper. Williamsport: Lycoming College, 1980.

Russell Mary L. "History of the Music of Williamsport." Unpublished Master's thesis. Pennsylvania State University, 1957.

Sanderson, W.H. "The Life and Times of William Hepburn." *Journal of the Lycoming County Historical Society* 6 (1969): 6–11.

Sipe, C. Hale. *Indian Chiefs of Pennsylvania*. Lewisburg, PA: Ziegler Printing, 1927.

Taber, Thomas T. III. *Williamsport Lumber Capital*. Williamsport, PA: Thomas T. Taber III, 1995.

Tozier, Gladys. "The Ring of the Axe and Whir of the Saw." *Journal of the Lycoming County Historical Society* 7.2 (1971): 13–22.

Van Doren, Carl. *Secret History of the American Revolution*. New York: Viking Press, 1941.

Wallace, Paul A.W. *Indians in Pennsylvania*. Harrisburg: Pennsylvania Historical and Museum Commission, 1961.

Williamsport Sun, 1801–1955.

Williamsport Sun-Gazette, 1801–2001.

Williamsport Junior League. *The West Fourth Street Story*. Williamsport: Grit Publishing, 1975.

INDEX

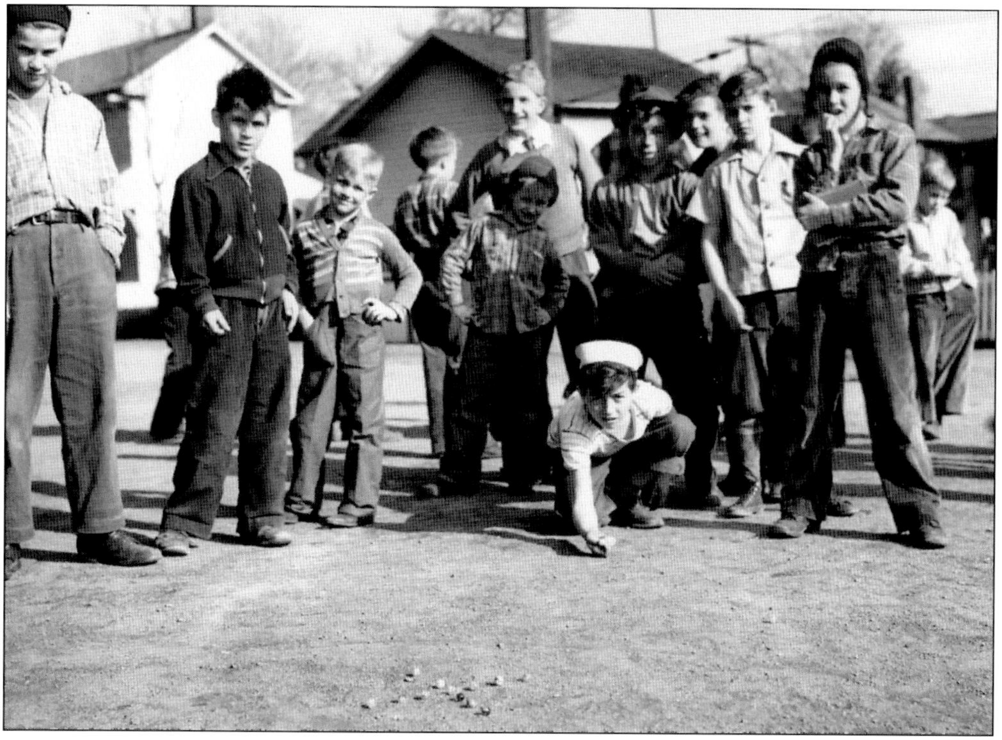

A young boy carefully prepares for a shot during a marble competition at Memorial Park during the 1940s. (WSG/GRIT.)